PRAI

THE FIRST-TIME

"Another Mike Weinberg Classic. The powerful principles in *The First-Time Manager: Sales* helped me secure my first sales leadership position, and this essential playbook will help any leader build a solid foundation and get out of the gate fast. Candid stories, actionable advice, and humorous blunt talk all rooted in the 'simple' fundamentals we've come to appreciate from Mike. It's not hard to call this a must-read for both seasoned and new managers!"

—**DREW ELLIS,**
vice president of Midmarket North America, SAP

"In *The First Time Manager: Sales*, Mike Weinberg has delivered a comprehensive playbook covering not only everything a new sales manager needs but that veteran managers should revisit frequently. Elements that resonated with me immediately were the focus on fundamentals amid the rise of so many technical toys and the absolute criticality of seeking to be the hero-maker, not the hero. Since reading it, I have already instituted open office hours and 1:1 sessions focused solely on accountability, and I am seeing immediate impact!"

—**CARSON HEADY,**
managing director of Microsoft Health & Life Sciences
and author of *Salesman on Fire*

"A refreshing and succinct take on all the fundamentals required for being a great sales manager. Mike Weinberg expertly debunks many management fads and returns coaching, accountability, and time management to their rightful place as the key difference makers. Sales managers ignore these lessons at their own peril, and the wise will successfully apply these practical insights for both their benefit and their team's!"

—**JOHN P. KANAN,**
senior partner of Bain & Company

"Mike Weinberg has done it again! Like his other heavily highlighted books with dozens of folded page corners, *The First-Time Manager: Sales* sits on my desk within easy reach. After twenty-plus years in sales leadership, Mike somehow finds ways to remind me of the 'simple' principles that are so easily forgotten. This is a fantastic, fast read with easily understandable processes for both new and seasoned sales managers."

—**DANA UPSHAW,**
chief growth officer of Recom

"The world's leading authority on sales management has done it again—this time imparting wisdom specifically to the first-time manager. Deploying his trademark practical truth-telling, Mike Weinberg offers a stark reminder of what really matters in sales, and in chapter 9 he shares the formula for becoming the 'I'd-lay-down-in-traffic-for-them' kind of leader we all hope to become. Deploy this approach to balance hard facts and empathy to lead your team to victory time and time again."

—**JEFF BAJOREK,**
author, consultant, and host of the *Rethink the Way You Sell* podcast

"In an engaging, conversational manner, *The First Time Manager: Sales* provides the essential 'how to' guide to make even the rawest recruit a stunning new manager. This is now mandatory reading for all recently appointed sales managers and critical review material for our veteran managers. Executives who manage sales managers will find this book important in their job of coaching coaches. If you are short on time, read, memorize, and execute just chapter 3. It embodies the essence of great sales management."

—**DR. CHRIS NELSON,**
chief executive officer of Kemin Industries

"If the path to excellence is paved with mastery of the fundamentals, then there is no better guide than *The First-Time Manager: Sales*. Once again, Mike Weinberg has delivered a masterpiece in his simple yet pragmatic approach that is a roadmap for any sales leader, new or experienced, to follow. Do what is in this book and you cannot fail. Do it well, and you will flourish."

—**MIKE JEFFREY,**
vice president of HCM Solution Sales, Paychex

"Mike Weinberg has a masterful way of taking the overwhelming weight placed on sales managers to produce results and narrowing down to the key strategies that will create quick and lasting impact. This book is the ultimate kick-start for any new leader and will serve as an empowering reality

check for a developed sales organization. Embrace these core principles, and your sales pipeline and results will thank you." —**EMILIA HUDDLE,**
vice president of sales of MedPro Systems

"I recommend this book to any salesperson contemplating a move into management . . . No-nonsense advice on what it takes to win as a sales leader. I love the focus of chapters 3 and 4 on accountability and coaching. *The First-Time Manager: Sales* will become required reading for students in our program. Another winner from Mike Weinberg!"

—**DAWN DEETER, PHD,**
professor, distinguished chair, and director of
Kansas State National Strategic Selling Institute

"Mike Weinberg and I share a passion for coaching and are driven to see others experience transformational change. We agree that mastery of the fundamentals is the key to long-term success. I am humbled and honored to be included in this book and believe that managers will significantly up their coaching game (and their team members' results) by implementing the principles in chapter 4." —**BRIAN FOGT,**
director of instruction of Bellerive Country Club
and *Golf Digest* #1-rated golf teacher in Missouri

"I feel like Mike Weinberg wrote this little book for me. It is so packed with actionable content that, from front cover to back, I was taking notes and blocking time on the calendar to implement my takeaways! My team at Salesforce is already benefiting from two best practices Mike preaches—the candidate interview framework and spending more time with our best people." —**JASON THOMAS,**
vice president of sales of Salesforce

"This power-packed book is not simply for sales managers; it's a must-read for any first-time people leaders! Mike's practical wisdom, clear guidance, and, most importantly, his straightforward approach to selfless, authentic leadership will not only help you capture the hearts and minds of your team but will put you on the path to driving outstanding results."

—**ASHLEY SCHUELER,**
senior leader of sales training of Vermeer Corporation

"The sales manager is one of the most important roles in an organization, yet it has an extremely high rate of failure because, until now, there has been no framework to teach newly promoted salespeople how to transition effectively into the manager role and maximize the results of their teams. Mike Weinberg knocks it out of the park with *The First-Time Manager: Sales* and provides new managers the perspective, approach, and disciplines needed to build and optimize a high-performing sales team. Read. This. Book."

—**GREG STANLEY,**
president of Accelerant Consultants

"This book will help you help your sales team members to become heroes. The routines in accountability, coaching, and connecting on the heart level outlined will set the standard of excellence in sales to win big. I took Mike Weinberg's advice to heart when I started my journey as a first-time manager in sales and have not stopped using it since!"

—**DENNIS BEEN,**
global leader of sales development of Pyrotek

"Managers who intentionally engage at the heart level foster an environment where their people become emotionally invested in their work, put forth more effort, and take more ownership of their results. In *The First-Time Manager: Sales*, Mike Weinberg offers frontline managers the foundational roadmap to developing their people and building trusted relationships with team members that ultimately lead to sales prosperity."

—**LARRY LEVINE,**
author of *Selling from the Heart*

THE FIRST-TIME MANAGER SALES

THE FIRST-TIME MANAGER

SALES

MIKE WEINBERG

HarperCollins Leadership

An Imprint of HarperCollins

Published by HarperCollins Leadership, an imprint of HarperCollins Focus LLC.

ISBN 978-1-4002-4152-1 (eBook)
ISBN 978-1-4002-4151-4 (TP)

Library of Congress Control Number: 2023931457

Printed in the United States of America
24 25 26 27 28 LBC 8 7 6 5 4

For my parents,

Thank you for loving me unconditionally, providing
a lifetime of support and encouragement, and being
the amazing parents and grandparents you are.

CONTENTS

INTRODUCTION

I WAS BEYOND HONORED THAT HarperCollins Leadership invited me to author this title for the expanded series of *First-Time Manager* books and could not be more excited to help you successfully launch your sales management career.

The transition into sales management is a unique and challenging one. As you will soon read in chapter 2, the role of leading a sales team often feels like the exact opposite of the job that precedes it—the individual contributor salesperson. Remarkably, there are precious few reputable resources to help first-time sales managers make this massive transition, which served as great motivation to pour energy into crafting the book you are holding.

I want you to know, before even diving into *The First-Time Manager: Sales*, that the mysterious journey of a brand-new sales manager is not unfamiliar territory to me. Quite to the contrary, as you'll discover in chapter 7, my entry into sales management was anything but smooth and successful despite my having been a top-producing salesperson in multiple organizations and having just concluded an amazing four years coaching and consulting sales teams. I understand the first-time manager's challenges firsthand because I suffered through them, and the irony is not lost on me that the very same person who struggled so mightily in his first sales leadership role years later authored *Sales Management. Simplified* and now spends most of his waking hours helping companies around the globe increase sales management effectiveness.

An overarching theme running through this book is that *you* are the key—the key to your team's sales success. I truly believe that you have accepted one of most important jobs in the entire economy—leading a group of people responsible for driving the top line of the business. As the key person at the center of this critical cog in the organization, you have the unique opportunity to affect not just the livelihood of the business but the careers and lives of your team members. That's a substantial responsibility, and the frameworks and best practices presented here will prepare and empower you to lead exceedingly well.

You will quickly realize, however, as you progress through the chapters that much of the advice is counterintuitive, and many of the topics, while not considered trendy, are absolutely critical for success in sales management. Said more simply, topics that are quite popular on LinkedIn are often not that useful when actually attempting to lead a sales team, and while it seems that everyone in the sales-improvement industry wants to talk about cool new hacks, tricks, and tools, much of what I present will intentionally feel quite old school. For example, in chapters 3 and 4, I make the strong case that your two most important jobs are first, ensuring that your people do their jobs, and second, helping your team members do their jobs better. Simply mastering these two critical functions will propel you into the upper echelon of sales managers—guaranteed. Holding salespeople accountable and investing time to work alongside them are the two highest-payoff sales management activities. While not sexy topics, executing these fundamentals really well is what truly drive sales results.

Chapter 5 waves a giant yellow caution flag pointing out the causes, and awful consequences that result, when sales managers fall into the very common trap of attempting to do their salespeople's jobs. Instead of leading, coaching, and holding team members accountable, many managers attempt to play the hero and insert themselves directly into every imaginable situation. This approach is neither scalable nor sustainable and does untold damage to the culture, the salespeople, and to the often well-intentioned manager.

The three critical components of smart sales-talent management are covered in chapters 6, 7, and 8. From precise job descriptions that attract the right candidates and repel the poseurs, to radically improving your interview game, you will gain a passion for getting the right people on your team. Executing the counterintuitive counsel in chapter 7 will ensure that you have more fun and drive more results as a manager. And after finishing chapter 8 you will be more comfortable and confident in quickly addressing struggling sellers, and you will never again turn a blind eye toward underperformance.

Over the past few years I have become more keenly aware that sales managers rarely comprehend the enormous head and heart space they occupy in their team members. Chapter 9 is devoted to helping managers appreciate this weighty responsibility and to use all of that mental and emotional bandwidth they consume wisely (for both the salesperson's and their own good).

Chapter 10 offers up one last critical, counterintuitive tip and a caution, which is that it's often the new manager's overzealous desire to get off to a fast start that creates a longer, slower ramp-up period. You will discover why it is imperative to slow down in order to speed up, and you'll also receive practical, powerful input from two favorite, wildly talented, and successful sales leaders offering their perspectives to maximize your early effectiveness as a first-time manager.

There is no more important job than being entrusted to lead a team responsible for driving revenue. I am truly excited for your new venture into sales management and thrilled you have chosen this book to help you become a world-class sales manager! Let's dive in.

THE FIRST-TIME MANAGER SALES

1

YOUR JOB IS THE MOST CRITICAL JOB IN THE BUSINESS

CONGRATULATIONS, SALES MANAGER! You now have the single most critical job in the entire company.

That statement is not an exaggeration. You have been entrusted to lead the team responsible for driving revenue. What could be more important than that?

I'm not trying to be dramatic. Or scare you. Or even sell you a book (since you've already purchased it). It's just the simple truth: the entire organization depends on you and your sales team doing your job and doing it well. Without a top line there is no bottom line, and I'm sure you've heard this common expression: nothing happens until somebody sells something. So, welcome to sales management. Everyone, and I mean everyone, is counting on you to succeed.

My passion, or my *why*, as it has become trendy to say, is helping salespeople and sales teams win more New Sales. That's why I do what I do. It's why I get on as many airplanes and stay in as many hotels as I do every year. It's why I blog, host events, publish a podcast, and write books. I love sales. I bleed sales. I am a proud salesperson. And there's nothing (in business) I'd rather do than work with salespeople to increase their effectiveness at developing new business and closing more New Sales.

But as much as I absolutely love working directly with sales teams, I cannot deny what I have observed over the past fifteen years:

> The sales manager is the key to creating a healthy, high-performance sales culture and driving long-term sales results.

So much so that I begin every sales leadership workshop, talk, training session, cohort, or keynote with this statement:

> You are the key.

That is exactly why over the past decade I have shifted the focus of my coaching, speaking, and consulting practice to spend more and more time with sales managers and executives. It's the multiplier effect. When we get sales management right, everything changes.

And if there is one takeaway I desperately want you to grasp from this first chapter in a book for first-time sales managers, it is the overarching theme that you, the sales team leader, are truly the key to sales success.

Now don't read more into this than I have written. In no way am I saying that your salespeople can't do better. Oh, believe me. They can do better! Your salespeople could certainly be more strategic in targeting of accounts. They could sharpen their messaging (story) and be more compelling with their language. They could prospect with more passion and persistence. They could take better control of their calendars to spend more time proactively pursuing new business and less time babysitting their favorite accounts or looking for customer service fires to extinguish. For sure, they could be more consultative on sales calls, and they could ask more and better questions, listen more intently, present with more power, more adeptly overcome objections. . . .

Oh yes. They can do better. And while I love to help sales teams improve in all of these areas, and a large chunk of my firm's business and my personal income comes from training salespeople, I am compelled to share this with you because It. Is. The. Truth. All the sales training (today many companies call this "enablement") in the world will not make a significant impact on sales results, and the culture required to sustain those results in the long term, if you (and your company) do not get the big sales management things right.

Are you tracking with me? That's one heckuva statement from the person who authored *New Sales. Simplified* and is best known for his work training sales teams. Said even more strongly, I am declaring, without hesitation or reservation, that sales training (enablement) is, for the most part, a useless, giant waste of time and money *unless* we master the fundamentals of sales management—culture, accountability, talent management (keeping our best people on our team happy and productive, while also quickly identifying and addressing underperformers), compensation, celebration, team meetings, and strategically guiding sellers in the right direction.

So before we dive headlong into helping you grasp these all-important fundamentals, let's define and clarify exactly what your job as sales manager is and what it is not.

2

YOUR NEW JOB (AS MANAGER) IS NOTHING LIKE YOUR OLD JOB (IN SALES)

BUCKLE UP BECAUSE IT'S VERY POSSIBLE that nobody has yet shared this important truth with you, so I will put it on the table right here at the outset as you begin your sales management journey. The title of this chapter is not hyperbole. It is a fact. Your new job is nothing like your old job.

My new sales manager friend, to quote the great Marshall Goldsmith, "What got you here won't get you there."

Almost the only similarity between your former job in sales and your new job as sales manager is the word *sales*! In many ways the roles are polar opposites, and the faster you recognize and adapt to this reality, the smoother your transformation will be into a highly effective sales leader.

• • •

RESPONSIBLE FOR ONE VERSUS RESPONSIBLE FOR MANY

When people ask me why I went into sales and why I love sales, it's easy to offer up a straightforward three-part answer: Freedom. Fun. Financial Reward. And of these three compelling reasons, the first one trumps the other two.

I love freedom, and there is nothing better than being judged by what I produce, not by how much I work. Sales is about results and to the successful salesperson, nothing beats the satisfaction (or confidence) that comes from putting up numbers . . . from exceeding your sales goal. There is something truly unique about life as a highly successful individual contributor. For the most part, you are responsible for one person—yourself! And the freedom from not having to play the corporate political game or caring what people think about when you arrive or what time you leave the office can be life-giving. It certainly was for me.

When you're in sales your job is crystal clear. As long as you are good with being judged by an objective scorecard, there is amazing freedom. Said another way, salespeople can maintain a simple, singular focus—their own performance.

But the shift to sales management changes everything. And I mean *everything.* Not only are you no longer just responsible for yourself, truthfully, "you" are no longer even viewed as an "individual." That is a weighty reality and a burden that many new managers are not prepared to shoulder.

WINNING THROUGH YOUR PEOPLE

The mindset shift required to succeed in management is massive.

There is no plainer way to say this. While individual contributors win on their own, sales managers win through their people. Just pause for a few moments to reflect on the enormity of that statement—and the implications.

WHILE INDIVIDUAL CONTRIBUTORS WIN ON THEIR OWN, SALES MANAGERS WIN THROUGH THEIR PEOPLE.

What are the implications of having to shift from winning on your own to winning through your people? Think about it from both philosophical and practical perspectives.

Let's jump right in and start with a biggie—*ego*. In sales, a healthy, dare I say even a bit *oversized*, ego is a good thing. But in a management role, not so much. A strong ego, which is actually beneficial for the individual producer, can be deadly when it manifests itself in a leader.

It is fine when a salesperson craves the spotlight, seeks the credit, and is energized and motivated by recognition. We all understand this. In fact, it's not just accepted; in many environments it is encouraged. But the same is not true for the manager. The leader with an oversized ego gets old very fast. Who wants to work for someone who is constantly seeking a pat on the back? Or worse, is looking to grab the applause and limelight? Nothing kills a culture or sales team's morale faster than an egotistical, self-promoting manager acting like the hero.

Beyond the need to subdue one's ego, there is another significant philosophical shift required for transitioning into sales management.

FROM SELFISH TO SELFLESS

When I moved from top-producing salesperson into sales management, the biggest and most difficult adjustment stemmed from the necessitated shift to a *selfless* approach from one that was very much *selfish.*

I often remind sellers that the word *selfish* gets a bad rap. From the time we are little, we are instructed not to be selfish. We should share. Share our cookies. Share our toys. And now in the business world we are constantly reminded to be good corporate citizens, team players, and collaborators.

It all sounds nice, but my strong (and contrarian) message to individual salespeople looking to produce more results is that they actually need to become more selfish, but in a positive way. The highest-performing sellers are what I call *selfishly productive.* They own their calendars. They focus like mad on their highest-payoff activities that create, advance, and close (the only three verbs that matter) sales! They have no problem saying no to others who are looking to put extra work on their plates. They smile and respond with a definitive "no, thank you" when asked to volunteer for the holiday party committee.

The uncomfortable truth that most HR people don't want to hear is that the majority of highest-performing salespeople are not the collaborative team players they write about in flowery job descriptions. They are selfish sales killers who have mastered the ability to stay laser focused on the precious few high-value activities that move the needle and drive results.

This was instinctive for me, a top-producing sales hunter. When I was in full-driver go-mode, I figuratively put on blinders like a thoroughbred racehorse so I would not get distracted or diverted from running the race. And when I was executing a calendar time block doing outbound new business development, I'd go as far as putting a sign on my door (or the back of my chair before I had an office with a door) that said, On the Sell Phone—Do Not Disturb.

When you are in sales, time is your most precious commodity, and once it is spent or wasted, it's gone. So if you were a super-successful salesperson before moving into sales management, it's a pretty safe bet to assume you also became highly skilled at protecting your time. And while the discipline of blocking time is still very much relevant in a management role, it looks very different in its application.

One of the greatest challenges I observe with newly promoted managers is making that shift from *individual contributor/closed door* mentality to a *team leader/open door* posture. While it's easy to read about and intellectually grasp this required shift, actually adopting this new approach is infinitely harder. At least it was for me and many of the new sales leaders I have coached.

Here are a few practical, easy-to-implement tips to help you win through your people and assist with your successful transition from selfish to selfless:

1. **Office hours**—It doesn't get simpler than this. Block a couple hours per week for holding "office hours" similar to the practice of college professors. Let your team know you are blocking this time specifically for them. Your office is open (whether in person or virtually), and you are encouraging your people to pop in (or call you or hop into a Zoom or Teams meeting) as desired. You have no

preset agenda. Your "door" is open, and you are available to tackle any topic.

You may be shocked at how highly productive these office hours become and how much your team members appreciate the opportunity to bring their questions, challenges, or possibly even their loneliness to you. These sessions are mutually edifying and energizing, which is why it is surprising that more managers (in every area of the company) don't make time for such a simple, rewarding, and productive activity. I often offer office hours for cohort groups I'm leading, and I have yet to walk away from one of these sessions disappointed or thinking it was a waste of time.

2. **Schedule One-on-One Coaching and Observation Sessions**—We will dive deeper into the best practices of coaching and working *alongside* your people in chapter 4, but for now, let's start here: without a doubt, one of your highest-impact activities as a manager is working one-on-one with your team members. Often just *being with them* is valuable in and of itself, let alone having the opportunity to share observations, offer feedback, or coach them on skills, and so on.

   Too many managers cheat themselves (and their people) of the benefit from intentional coworking sessions with their salespeople. They just don't make the time to proactively cycle through working with each of their team members. Sure, managers jump in when there is a crisis or big opportunity or when someone is struggling. But they are missing out on the tremendous benefits, for both themselves and sales team members, that result from simply spending time with them while they are doing their job. My coaching to you is to go beyond just stating that you believe that coaching and observing your people is a priority. Demonstrate it! Before your calendar fills up with other (less essential) tasks, get in there first and schedule one-on-one time with each of your people, even your very best sales reps.

3. **Show Love and Attention to Your Salespeople as if They Are Your Customers**—This is not an original thought. For years, I've heard strong leaders speak about the importance of treating team members as if they are their customers. As sellers, we all understand the importance of retaining and growing customer relationships. As managers, the same applies to our people!

   Practically speaking, this means demonstrating that we care with actions. We check in, not to micromanage, but because we care. We initiate contact to let them know we are thinking about them, not just to ask for an order. When we see something in the news, or about their favorite sports team, we text message them the link and say, "This made me think of you."

   Relationships matter. Remember, we are leading humans, not robots. And as we will examine further in chapter 9, as managers, we take up way more emotional and mental bandwidth in our people's hearts and minds than we tend to be aware. That's a weighty responsibility worthy of further exploration.

   For now, let me propose this practical tip: create a little journal to capture notes on each of your people's personal favorites—hobbies, interests, sports teams, or family milestones. Every so often, peruse that journal and then find a current event or news story that would interest your team member. It may seem trite, but they will not think it's trivial that you remembered a kid's birthday or the anniversary of a parent's passing. It shows that you care and are interested in that person.

And follow your people on social media so you are aware of key happenings in their lives. This is not stalking. This is smart! Just today as I'm writing this chapter, a colleague posted on Instagram about dropping off his daughter at college. It gave me the chance to send a text message encouraging him that every tear he sheds today is beautiful, and it provided an opportunity for us to bond over a common experience. That's what caring, empathetic humans do—they demonstrate that they care. And that is exactly what the best leaders do too.

THE TENDENCY TO DO INSTEAD OF LEAD, COACH, AND HOLD ACCOUNTABLE

Before we look ahead to mastering the most important aspect of managing a sales team (ensuring that your people actually do their jobs), I have one final thought on what your new job is *not*.

The very best salespeople are always in action. In fact, they are proactive. They understand that their job is to *do*. It falls squarely on them to get things done. They are the ones responsible for creating, advancing, and closing sales opportunities, and they *own* the outcome. They look in the mirror and say to themselves, *It's on me; I've got this.* They don't point fingers or make excuses. Again, the very best sellers own the reality that if it needs to get done, they are the ones to make it happen—even if that requires taking heroic action.

While it's all well and good when sellers see themselves as *heroes*, very often new sales managers bring that same hero mentality with them into their new job as team leader. It makes sense that they do this. A big part of the reason they were so successful as individual contributors is because they played the hero role well. They did whatever was necessary to win, and it's only natural that they would continue with that mentality as managers.

The problem however is that the sales manager's job is not to play sales team superhero. Nowhere in any legitimate sales team leader job description does it list this as an expectation: "When in doubt, jump in and do your people's jobs for them." But, because that's exactly what most of us did in our sales roles, as managers we default to what worked so well for us as sellers. We take over. We insert ourselves in the middle of every deal. We *do* whatever we deem necessary to win.

While that worked marvelously for us in our old roles, it creates a disastrous and unsustainable situation when we are supposed to be *leading* a team. Really, really bad things happen when sales managers view themselves as sales team hero and attempt to do everyone's job instead of leading, coaching, and holding people accountable. The manager playing sales team hero is neither scalable nor sustainable. It also creates about a dozen other problems and traps that damage culture, run off top talent, and make the sales manager's life a living hell. My hope is this stern warning has caused you to pause and reflect on whether you may have already started down this dangerous path so early in your management career. I've got more for you on the causes and implications of managers playing team hero and how to avoid falling into this career-limiting and quality-of-life-damaging behavior in chapter 5.

3

YOUR NUMBER ONE JOB IS ENSURING THAT YOUR PEOPLE DO THEIR JOBS

AS A NEW SALES MANAGER, I was completely blindsided by the reality that salespeople need to be held accountable and that a really large percentage of the job was ensuring that my people were doing their jobs.

Looking back, I now smile in amusement reflecting on my naivete. I was excited about my first chance to serve in a leadership capacity. I was energized by the opportunity to invest in the people entrusted to me. With great anticipation I looked forward to coaching salespeople—something I had always loved doing. But somehow, someway, as a brand-new first-time manager, I was completely unaware that people, particularly *salespeople,* needed to be managed . . . and a big part of *management* was holding people accountable.

Let's be honest. Nobody really wants to be thought of as a *manager.* A coach? Sure. A leader or mentor? Absolutely. Don't we all aspire to leadership? But a manager, no thank you!

By definition, moving into a management role requires actually *managing* our people. Crazy, I know. But don't for a second begin to equate appropriate management, which includes holding people accountable for doing their job and achieving results, with micromanagement. Good sales management and proper accountability could not be more different from micromanagement!

As I flashback almost two decades from my baptism by fire into sales management and then fast-forward to today, the irony is not lost on me that I spend more time tackling the topic of accountability than any other when I speak with client sales leaders. Let me repeat that statement for emphasis: when I am coaching, speaking, facilitating workshops or cohorts, or training sales managers, no single topic gets more time, attention, and bandwidth than accountability. Why is that? Because our most important job is making sure that the people responsible for driving revenue into our businesses are doing their job. Period. Full stop.

OUR MOST IMPORTANT JOB IS MAKING SURE THAT THE PEOPLE RESPONSIBLE FOR DRIVING REVENUE INTO OUR BUSINESSES ARE DOING THEIR JOB.

ACCOUNTABILITY IS NOT A SEXY TOPIC

If you search today's sales literature, particularly on LinkedIn, you will find very little written on the topic of accountability. Accountability is not a sexy topic. It doesn't get a lot of attention or attract a lot of eyeballs. How to *coach* salespeople, now that is a popular topic. And for the past five or so years, *enabling* sellers has become all the rage. When people in the sales-improvement industry are looking for views, likes, and clicks, they write articles titled something like "What's in Your *Tech Stack*?"

There are several reasons that *sales enablement* remains a hot topic. First and foremost, there are hundreds, if not thousands, of sales tool vendors pouring millions and millions of dollars into marketing their solutions. Their mission is simple and transparent. Every one of these providers is trying to create FOMO (fear of missing out) in you. They, and their venture capital financial backers, desperately want you to believe that for you and your sales team to succeed, you/they must have the latest, greatest tools and toys available. Said simply, if you're not achieving optimal sales results right now it is because you don't have their slick shiny new tool in your tech stack.

Believe me, I get it. I understand FOMO with the best of them, particularly when it has to do with my golf game. The only people on this planet better at marketing new toys than sales tool vendors are golf equipment manufacturers! Why in the world would I want to do the tedious, unsexy work on something as fundamental as fixing my grip or perfecting my takeaway/backswing when I'm constantly being seduced by advertisements offering me more yardage and more forgiveness from artificial intelligence–infused new driver heads? Come on. I mean, what's more fun, watching new golf club reviews on YouTube or doing the heavy lifting by practicing the fundamentals over and over and over? Why should I go see my coach, take a lesson, and get really good at executing the basics when it's a whole lot more fun (and easier) to just order new equipment? Besides, these golf equipment brands have convinced me that there is no way I can optimize my game without their latest and greatest creations. Not only am I seduced by the shortcut they are offering for adding twenty yards to my drive and lowering my score, but they have also succeeded in convincing me that without their fancy new equipment, I will indeed be missing out.

Those exact same sentiments are what mess us up as sales leaders. We get distracted by shiny objects and potential quick fixes, and we fall for the hype. But don't read more into this than I'm actually writing. In no way am I suggesting that sales tools are bad or unnecessary. Your team may very well benefit from being better *enabled*. But this I can share with absolute certainty: I have never seen a sales manager or sales team fail because they were missing the latest and greatest tools and technology. So, similar to how I must be careful not to get sucked into the hype of what new golf clubs would do for my game, I offer that you would be well advised to be wary of the false promises from sales tool vendors proclaiming that they have the fix for all that ails your sales!

I HAVE NEVER SEEN A SALES MANAGER OR SALES TEAM FAIL BECAUSE THEY WERE MISSING THE LATEST AND GREATEST TOOLS AND TECHNOLOGY.

Another common trap for new managers is the false belief that coaching salespeople serves the same function as holding them accountable. This all-too-common misconception is exactly why I am being so specific in the titling of this chapter and the next.

Holding your sales team members accountable for doing their jobs (producing results) and coaching them to do their jobs better are two completely distinct aspects of our role. Yet I would argue that they are our two highest-impact, highest-payoff activities as managers.

There is a very specific reason we are tackling accountability and mastering the one-on-one manager-salesperson accountability meeting before we address coaching our people. Mentoring and coaching (investing in our people) are hugely important. My caution here, however, based on years of experience helping increase sales management effectiveness, stems from the observation that most of us in sales management prefer to coach. Given the choice, we would choose a coaching conversation over a results-focused accountability session. Why? Because we were previously so successful at selling, it is only natural for us to default to either "modeling" the behavior that we're looking for or "coaching" it.

It is understandable why we do this, and I get that our motivation is good. Our hearts are in the right place. We want to help. We want to see our people succeed, and that desire is pure and beautiful! But our urge to help often supersedes our willingness to hold our people accountable. And for us, and our team, to succeed in the long term, we must have sellers carrying the burden of owning their outcomes, their results. The responsibility falls on managers to make it exceedingly clear to our people that they, and they alone, are on the hook for producing results and hitting their sales goals. That is why our first and most important job is ensuring that our people are doing their jobs! Once we have established a high-performance, results-focused culture with accountability as a central core value, then we quickly proceed to helping our salespeople become better at their jobs. Accountability precedes coaching just as this chapter precedes the next.

ACCOUNTABILITY IS GOOD AND GOOD SALESPEOPLE WANT TO BE HELD ACCOUNTABLE

Before getting into approaches and techniques for creating a culture of accountability and conducting highly effective one-on-one accountability meetings, let's address a common misconception. Accountability is a good thing. It's not dirty, wrong, demotivating, or politically incorrect to review results with our salespeople or to publish, post, or distribute sales reports. Please go back and reread that last sentence, because it is absolutely critical that as a new manager you believe and own the concept that holding people accountable is good, not bad.

I've worked with countless newer managers who come into the role carrying unhelpful mental baggage around the topic of accountability. They tell me that they're uncomfortable holding salespeople accountable because they haven't yet "earned the right." Or they say things like, "I feel that I need to build the relationship with my team before sitting down with them to review results against their goals." Or they say that as a rookie manager they don't feel ready to hold a veteran salesperson's feet to the fire.

I get it. And while I fully understand the hesitancy and appreciate their desire to build solid relationships with team members, that doesn't make their false belief any more correct. In other words, just because as a new manager you don't feel ready or positive about having data/fact/results-based conversations with your team members, that does not make the act of having these conversations any less important—or effective!

I have good news if the paragraphs above created a touch of anxiety because they describe you. Most salespeople want to be held accountable. They understand that sales is about results. Good salespeople appreciate it when the person leading them communicates clear expectations and helps keep them abreast of where they stand on achieving their goals.

Let's just call it like it is. The best salespeople are competitive. They keep score. In fact, the very fact that there is a scorecard (a sales report) motivates them. True salespeople want to be reminded where they stand against their goal and where they rank against teammates. That's part of what drives them.

But would you like to guess which salespeople don't like it when the sales report is published? Exactly. Who on your team will not appreciate the regular, scheduled, brief, results-focused sit-down I'm about to prescribe? You got it. Those whose results stink.

As one of my favorite, most talented, and most effective sales executive clients often says, "Struggling salespeople love to talk about everything but their results." And that, my new manager friend, is exactly why it is imperative that we adopt a cadence of regularly scheduled, formal, one-on-one results- and progress-focused accountability meetings if we expect to create a healthy, high-performance sales culture and drive more New Sales.

ACCOUNTABILITY IS BEST DONE ONE-ON-ONE

I am a huge proponent of well-run sales team meetings and believe they play an important role in creating a healthy culture, building camaraderie, fostering competition, sharing best practices, brainstorming challenges, envisioning, aligning, training, equipping, and energizing salespeople. But, and a big but, in this author's opinion, they are *not* the ideal venue for holding people accountable.

Others will disagree and argue vehemently that the regular sales meetings provide a wonderful opportunity to hold the team collectively accountable. They make the case that peer pressure is a positive force and that the desire to avoid being shamed in front of other team members motivates people to perform. Pardon my perspective, but I think that's a pathetic approach.

Please do not misread my guidance here. I am not arguing against posting sales reports during your team meetings and praising those who are succeeding. By all means, post the scorecard and highlight outstanding performance. That's a best practice and a far cry from what I see, or often hear about, many managers doing. Unfortunately, however, in some organizations it is common practice to call out underperformance right in the sales team meeting and force struggling salespeople to explain their poor results to their peers. My skin crawls even typing this. Sales is hard enough without being demeaned by your manager and publicly embarrassed in front of your peers. Who wants to work in that kind of environment?

I occasionally show funny movie clips to drive home a point when leading a sales or sales management workshop, and every once in a while, some smug, smarmy sales manager calls out from the back of the room and asks why I don't use clips from the classic (sad, dark) sales movie from 1992, *Glengarry Glen Ross*. If you are unfamiliar, it's a movie where Alec Baldwin plays the big-time sales executive brought in from *downtown* to turn around a struggling office, and in his first meeting with the sales team utters the now famous, oft-quoted line, "Put that coffee down! Coffee's for closers only." He then goes on a dehumanizing, expletive-laced tirade telling these salespeople in no uncertain terms that they are losers, and they better start selling more if they want to keep their jobs.

Why don't I show clips from this movie? Because there's not a redeeming thing about it. It's dark. It's wrong. It's not funny and it's not helpful. Frankly, it is the perfect example of how not to treat your people or lead your team meetings! And that opinion is coming from the person telling you that holding your people accountable for doing their job is your most important job.

One quick word about what sales team meetings are supposed to accomplish before we expand on the best practices for conducting highly effective one-on-one accountability meetings. There is a very simple binary question to evaluate whether your sales team meetings are productive. I regularly force sales managers to ask this simple question as a litmus test: yes or no? Do your salespeople leave the sales team meeting with more energy and better equipped to sell than when the meeting began? Again, it's binary. Either, yes, they leave with more energy and better equipped to succeed. Or, no, they leave with less energy and no better equipped to do their jobs well.

After several decades observing sales team meetings, I make the case, without reservation, that beating people up for poor performance and forcing team members to sit through their peers' detailed results and pipeline reviews neither energizes nor equips anyone. So instead of glamorizing and adopting Alec Baldwin's Hollywood approach, let's instead agree that this old adage is pretty solid advice: praise in public, criticize or correct in private.

A FOOLPROOF FRAMEWORK TO DRIVE ACCOUNTABILITY WITHOUT DEMOTIVATING OR MICROMANAGING YOUR TEAM

Lock in with me. What follows is the foolproof formula for creating a high-performance sales culture and ensuring your sales team members hit their number and maintain a full, healthy pipeline. And the best part? You can do this in fifteen minutes per month (or per week depending on your sales cycle) per salesperson, and do it without being a jerk, demotivating your sellers, or coming across as a micromanager.

This is not a pipe dream. I've seen it happen—time and time again across sales teams of all sizes in various industries. A regular, formal, scheduled one-on-one results- and pipeline-focused accountability meeting between the sales manager and each salesperson is the single highest-payoff, highest-impact sales management activity.

A REGULAR, FORMAL, SCHEDULED ONE-ON-ONE RESULTS- AND PIPELINE-FOCUSED ACCOUNTABILITY MEETING BETWEEN THE SALES MANAGER AND EACH SALESPERSON IS THE SINGLE HIGHEST-PAYOFF, HIGHEST-IMPACT SALES MANAGEMENT ACTIVITY.

When executed well, this one activity has the power to transform your sales culture and results.

Before tackling exactly how we do this, let's pause and unpack these three key words. Regular. Formal. Scheduled. Each is essential.

Regular refers to cadence. If I may borrow from the dictionary, this definition illustrates the meaning beautifully: "a constant or definite pattern, especially with the same space between individual instances." Regular, as in regular. Not the flavor of the day. Not every so often. Not just when you feel like it. Or when you have time. Or when someone is struggling. Not sporadically. Regular.

Formal, as in not casual. Planned. Professional. Not a hallway meeting. Not a quick text message. Not an email at

2:00 a.m. with a questionable tone. A formal sit-down meeting, whether it be in person, via phone, or virtual.

Scheduled means scheduled. It gets put on the calendar ahead of time. It is prioritized, not an afterthought. Scheduled, as in not a surprise. Both parties know the meeting is happening and come prepared.

The most popular chapter in my book *Sales Management. Simplified* is chapter 20, and I ask your indulgence as I borrow heavily from it, sharing this progression with you. It's the most powerful, effective, and simple concept I teach, and I have seen sales teams' cultures and results transformed simply from managers implementing the sales management accountability progression advocated there. Something wonderful and powerful transpires when managers review a salesperson's results, pipeline, and activity (in that specific order).

The very simple act of the sales manager sitting down formally with each salesperson every month—not for coaching, not to listen to excuses, not for reps to ask the manager to do their job but for the singular purpose of forcing the salesperson to answer for what they produced (results), what they are working on to produce results in the future (pipeline), and where they focused (activity) to generate and advance opportunities is transformative.

And this is my promise:

> No tool, no trick, and no training will produce the kind of sales lift created by you effectively doing your most important job: holding sellers accountable for doing their jobs.

THE ORDER MATTERS: RESULTS THEN PIPELINE THEN ACTIVITY

The order matters. We start our regular one-on-one accountability meetings focusing on results. Why? Because sales is about results. Results are what we most care about, so we start these accountability meetings with each of our salespeople by looking together with them at their individual results.

Results against goals. Results against last year. Results against other members of the team. Results.

We might look at total revenue, or number of new accounts opened or acquired, or gross margin percentage or gross margin dollars, or percentage of quota achieved, or market share gained, or growth over prior month or year, or cross-sell objectives, or account penetration, or specific product category results, or number of units moved, or relative ranking compared to other salespeople or divisions, or. . . .

You get the point. We spend the first few minutes of this short meeting looking at data. Actual numbers. Real results. Because something wonderful happens when we shine the light of truth on someone's actual performance in a one-on-one meeting. Salespeople are reminded in a stark and powerful way that their job is different from other jobs. They are not evaluated on the quantity of their work and not necessarily even their effort. I repeat: sales is about results, and that's why it is imperative that in our accountability meetings the burden for producing results falls squarely on the shoulders of the salesperson.

If the results are great, we praise and congratulate the salesperson before moving on to review the health of their pipeline. Alternatively, if the results are not there—the person missed the month, or is tracking behind where they should be for the quarter, or they did not achieve their territory or account growth objective, or their relative ranking compared to others on the team has dropped, and so on—then we ask a simple question: What happened? And for a moment, that salesperson feels the heat as you shine the light of truth on their performance as they find themselves in the uncomfortable position of having to rationalize or explain why their results were not up to par.

Again, this is a data-based, rational conversation. We are simply looking at actual numbers against goals and letting the numbers tell the story. There is no need to raise a voice or threaten or use bad words or deploy dramatic histrionics like Alec Baldwin in *Glengarry Glen Ross*. Our goal here is simple. We are concerned only with confronting our sellers with their own results. And if those results are wonderful, we briefly celebrate and praise them, and if the results fall short, we let them feel the weight of underperforming.

Regardless of whether the results are outstanding or poor, we don't linger on the results phase of this one-on-one accountability meeting because we cannot change the results. At this point, the results are old news; they're history. The numbers on the report are the numbers on the report, and there is nothing we can do to alter the past. But, and this is a big but, we certainly can affect future performance, which is why we spend the majority of this short meeting in the next two phases.

Following results, we move into the pipeline phase of this accountability meeting, where I advocate we spend the majority of our time.

Pipeline is a very common word in sales, but it means different things in different industries or companies. For simplicity's sake and for our purposes here, let's define *pipeline*, in a broad, generic sense. Let's consider the pipeline as the repository, or funnel, of all the potential deals/opportunities/proposals/quotes that a particular salesperson is working to close sales. And in this particular phase of the accountability meeting, we want to examine the health of a seller's pipeline with the goal of ensuring that it is healthy enough (sufficient) to ensure the salesperson will meet or exceed their sales goal.

I can make the case that a manager cannot spend enough time talking pipeline. The pipeline is everything. It's the lifeblood of the business! It is the future cash flow. As a sales leader, I am concerned with almost nothing more than pipeline health. A fat, healthy, balanced, moving pipeline of sales opportunities cures almost all sales problems. So during this phase of the accountability meeting, we dive in to examine overall pipeline health. Are there enough opportunities/deals in here to be exceedingly confident that the salesperson will hit their sales target for the month or the quarter or year? And along with total pipeline coverage, we also want to look at both *additions* and *advances*. Almost as much as I care about the overall size of the pipeline, I want to understand whether salespeople are both *creating* new opportunities at the top of the funnel and *advancing* existing opportunities that were already in the pipe.

Once more, let me remind us that this is a data-based conversation, and we are going to review real pipeline numbers (data) with each of our people. We are not interested in hearing about how excited they are, how hard they are working, or how much their customers supposedly love them. All we are looking at here are pipeline facts:

1. Is the pipeline sufficient? At your typical close rate, are there enough deals and dollars proposed for the salesperson to likely achieve their goal for the next period?

2. Are a sufficient number of new opportunities being added to the funnel? Is this salesperson creating enough new opportunities to keep the pipeline filled?
3. How many existing opportunities were advanced closer to a sale?

After reviewing total pipeline coverage, opportunities created, and opportunities advanced, both the sales manager and the salesperson now have a very clear indication of the objective health of this seller's pipeline. It's no longer about having a *gut feel;* it's about data. And if the data is good—sufficient number and size of opportunities to hit future goals—then this accountability meeting is over. There is no reason for a manager to examine a seller's activity level if the pipeline is healthy and chock full of good opportunities.

But if after reviewing this seller's pipeline, the manager is not comfortable with the data, there's no choice but to proceed to the activity phase of this one-on-one accountability meeting. Here's how I might transition from the pipeline into activity:

> Sarah, after digging into your pipeline with you, we can both see that there is not enough here for us to be comfortable that you will achieve your sales target for the upcoming period [week/month/quarter]. In fact, based on the data we are looking at, it is likely you will come up significantly short of your goal for the [week/month/quarter]. And with your pipeline this weak, you've left me no choice. We are going to have to dive into your activity level.

Now you are getting the feel for how this accountability progression works and why the order is so important. Results then pipeline then activity. Nobody wants to be asked about their activity, and honestly, we really shouldn't care about it either. What kind of adult enjoys being asked to account for how they spent their time? Yuck.

When salespeople understand the progression, and that the only time the manager will inquire about activity level is when forced to (due to poor pipeline health), they fully recognize that this is the furthest thing from micromanagement. They actually appreciate that we don't *want* to ask about activity, but when results are not there, and the pipeline is weak, as managers we have no choice.

FIVE KEYS TO MAXIMIZING THE EFFECTIVENESS OF YOUR ONE-ON-ONE ACCOUNTABILITY MEETINGS

1. THIS IS *YOUR* MEETING, NOT THE SALESPERSON'S MEETING.

Stay focused on the progression: review results (results against goal and relative performance versus other members of the sales team). Review overall health of the pipeline and ask about new opportunities created and existing opportunities advanced.

If results are not there and the pipeline is insufficient (not enough deals or not seeing new opportunities being added and existing opportunities advanced), then proceed to phase 3 of the progression: *activity*.

Stay focused on the progression and do not allow the salesperson to turn the tables or trick you into doing their job for them. This is not their meeting and not a coaching meeting (see next tip).

2. KEEP THIS ONE-ON-ONE MEETING SHORT AND FOCUS EXCLUSIVELY ON ACCOUNTABILITY.

While you absolutely should be observing, coaching, and mentoring your people, this one-on-one accountability meeting is neither the time nor the place. The most effective accountability meetings are short and focused on one thing—accountability! Resist the temptation to begin coaching your salesperson on specific opportunities or selling skills. Much of the transformative power from this one-on-one is derived from its purpose being singular: to put the salesperson on the hot seat with data/facts about their actual results, the health of their pipeline, and when necessary, their level of activity. This meeting will likely reveal coaching and training opportunities, but schedule one-on-one or team coaching sessions separately. Let this accountability stand out as the time that you and the salesperson focus exclusively on the accountability progression. This is how to keep the meeting to just ten or fifteen minutes per person and maximize its impact.

3. THIS IS A DATA (FACT-BASED) DIALOGUE, NOT AN EMOTIONAL CONFRONTATION.

This meeting absolutely can be conducted with a smile or a positive tone, even with salespeople who are struggling. There is no need for raised voices, bad words, or threats. Even managers who are conflict averse can effectively conduct this meeting without necessarily becoming confrontational. We are simply reviewing the facts, and the best accountability meetings are not based on feelings. The data speaks for itself, and it is not subjective. Follow the progression: Results. Pipeline. Activity.

4. DO NOT ALLOW THE STRUGGLING SALESPERSON TO PLAY THE MICROMANAGEMENT CARD.

Good management is not micromanagement! Don't allow the complaints or visible frustration from your underperforming/insecure salespeople who bristle at these one-on-one meetings to derail you. When a struggling salesperson pushes back against this type of meeting and plays the *micromanagement card*, complaining about your desire for increased visibility, particularly into activity, hold your ground:

- Remind the underperforming salesperson that the only reason you are asking hard questions about *activity* is because results are not what they should be, and this person's pipeline is weak/insufficient.
- Make it clear that you are "not cool with failing," and until results and pipeline health improve, you have no choice but to dig into activity.
- If they want to avoid your deep dive into their activity, they have a choice: they can either (a) hit their sales numbers and maintain a healthy pipeline of opportunities, or (b) they can go work somewhere else where it is okay to fail

5. DO NOT SKIP THIS ONE-ON-ONE MEETING (EVEN WITH TOP-PRODUCING SALESPEOPLE)!

This one-on-one results-, pipeline-, and activity-focused accountability meeting is your single highest-payoff sales management activity. If you are overbooked and overwhelmed, find something else to cancel or postpone. *Nothing* is more important for maintaining a high-performance culture than a laser focus on goals and results. You can find fifteen minutes per month per salesperson to conduct these one-on-ones. Prioritize these meetings above all else. I promise that you will see an immediate impact. As mentioned previously, when executed well, *this one activity has the power to transform your sales culture and your organization!*

BONUS RESOURCE

Watch a fifteen-minute video and download the free guide, *The Fastest Way to Increase Accountability, Reduce Complacency, and Create a High-Performance Sales Culture*, at mikeweinberg.com/thefirsttimemanager

4

YOUR SECOND MOST IMPORTANT JOB: HELPING YOUR PEOPLE DO THEIR JOBS BETTER

AS STRONGLY AS I ENCOURAGED YOU (in the last chapter) not to coach your salespeople during your one-on-one accountability meetings, that is the *only* time managers should not be coaching.

The reality is that helping your people do their jobs more effectively is both a hugely significant and satisfying part of your job as the sales manager. Yet what astonishes me on a daily basis is how few managers prioritize coaching and how many avoid it altogether.

Next to your regular, formal, scheduled sit-down to review results and progress with a salesperson, there is nothing that will increase sales results more than carving out time to proactively coach your people—both individually (one-on-one) and collectively (in team meetings).

In the (pre-internet) *old days,* developing salespeople was a source of great pride for most sales managers. It was common to hear managers bragging about mentoring rookies on their teams and developing them into superstars. Sales leaders would puff out their chests with pride and regale you with stories about how they invested in and turned around underperforming reps and turned them into top producers. Today, however, not so much.

WHERE DID ALL THE MANAGERS WHO COACH AND MENTOR GO?

It is incredibly rare for me to hear sales managers brag about how often and how effectively they're coaching their people. When I lead workshops on this topic, I often ask participants, "Where did all the sales mentors go?"

You see, I am a product of mentoring and coaching. If you look at the acknowledgment pages in my previous books, there are paragraphs and paragraphs where I thank dozens of individuals for investing in me. These mentors and managers shaped me. They built me. They modeled the way. They taught me how to pack my briefcase and how to pack for a business trip. How to dress. How to prepare for a sales call. How to present. How to go toe-to-toe sitting across the table from a senior executive.

I have strong memories of my first sales manager working alongside me. Even though it has been thirty years, I still distinctly remember that feeling of picking up Bob Smith (yes, that's his real name) at St. Louis Lambert Airport when he would fly in to spend a day or two with me. We'd spend long dinners talking about career goals and what it takes to grow into becoming a true professional. Then he'd get more specific and pepper me with constant questions about my territory and my account planning. Then he would dial in even more and ask detailed questions about a specific customer. Then he'd dive even deeper as we prepared for the next day's sales call with a key account. Bob left no stone unturned as he ensured we discussed the flow of the meeting, who was attending, what role we would each play, how we should pivot from reviewing business highlights to introducing our new product line, what obstacles and objections we might face, and how to overcome them.

So, my new sales manager friend, there is no way around this: so much of the success I achieved as a salesperson was because throughout my sales career, from newbie to veteran seller, I was coached by managers and executives who made the conscious decision that coaching was a priority. If you desire to achieve outrageous success as a manager and leader, then I encourage you to follow the example that was set for me. Prioritize helping your people do their job better. As stated in chapter 2, managers win through their people. If you want to win big you must help your people get better at winning!

THE CALENDAR DOES NOT LIE

People give a lot of lip service to things they believe others value. Said differently, most of us become pretty darn good at *talking about* things that we believe impress others. But talking is not the same as *doing*. This truism certainly applies to managers who spend a lot of time *talking about* coaching their people.

One of the most memorable sermon illustrations I ever heard had to do with the difference between what we say we value and how we actually live our lives. The pastor challenged us with this statement: if you really want to know what somebody truly values, don't listen to what they say; look at their calendar and their bank statement. Ouch.

Where we spend our precious time and dollars says a whole lot more about our true priorities than the words passing through our lips. So with that as the backdrop, may I ask you to pull up your calendar and scroll through the past thirty days examining where you spent (or wasted) your most precious, finite resource—your time? And just to drive this home a bit further, let's imagine that the sales development police accused you of not devoting enough time to proactively coaching and developing your team members and the case against you went to trial. When the prosecuting attorney projects your calendar up on the big screen in the courtroom for the jury to see, will there be enough evidence to prove, beyond a shadow of a doubt, that an appropriate percentage of your calendar was dedicated to developing your people and helping them do their jobs better?

Take a quick time-out right now. Close the book (pause the audio) and grab your calendar, whether it be electronic or old-school paper. Scroll back through Every. Single. Day. of the past month, or even two months if you'd like to get a better sample size. Keeping in mind that I am making the case that helping your people improve at doing their jobs is your second most important job as their manager, does the way you are spending your time reflect your agreement with my premise? Based on having this conversation with so many managers across such a variety of industries, my guess is that after reviewing your calendar, you may not be proud of what you discover, and you will be convicted that not enough of your precious time has been invested in this critical, high-payoff activity.

PREVENTING THE "URGENT" FROM DROWNING OUT THE IMPORTANT

I know that you know what you are about to read next. Regardless, you need to read this anyway: there is always too much to do. Always. Most sales managers, especially newer sales managers, live constantly on the edge of overwhelm, run around with their hair on fire, work way longer hours than their salespeople, process ridiculous numbers of email, get dragged to an obscene number of meetings, get asked for stupid amounts of data, and have more people vying for their attention than there is either mental bandwidth or calendar to give. What's even worse is that all of that *stuff* feels *urgent* at the moment it hits our desk, inbox, or smartphone.

MOST SALES MANAGERS, ESPECIALLY NEWER SALES MANAGERS, LIVE CONSTANTLY ON THE EDGE OF OVERWHELM.

I am not an idealist living in the land of make believe, nor am I an academician on a college campus simply preaching theory to you. As someone who walked in your shoes as a struggling new manager who felt like I could barely keep my head above water, and who has spent the past fifteen years as the coach, consultant, and trainer working alongside new managers, I get it. I totally get it. The demands on your time are real, and while the situation described in the previous paragraph is certainly not your fault, it is most definitely your problem. You did not dump all of this waste into the ocean, but you are forced to swim (live) in these polluted waters. So if you are committed to becoming a great manager, a strong leader who both develops people and drives the desired results, then it is imperative that you prioritize the precious few high-impact activities that truly move the needle.

Despite this truth being universally accepted, the reality in just about every organization is that when the crap hits the fan and the urgent begins overpowering the important, the Very. First. Thing. that sales managers, particularly first-time managers, cancel or postpone is the *proactive* coaching of their people!

I used a word very intentionally there: *proactive*. It's the proactive coaching that gets put off. The planned coaching. The nonurgent developmental coaching. That's the stuff we skip.

We're not fools. The *reactive* coaching doesn't get postponed. When there is a fire, we grab the fire extinguisher and put it out. If there's a crisis with a significant customer and one of our salespeople needs assistance, of course we jump right into the flames with them to help in whatever manner we can. Or if there's a huge presentation to deliver or a massive sales opportunity that deserves or requires management involvement, we magically become available in a nanosecond. Or if you've got a new person that can't find the restroom, log on to the network, or yet handle going one-on-one with a prospective customer, that's not someone you ignore. Of course not. When it's *urgent* or mission critical, we make time for it.

What's so dangerous about completing the types of *reactive* coaching I just outlined is that it makes us feel good. As managers, we get a feeling of satisfaction from helping to rescue a customer relationship that is in jeopardy or guiding team members as they prep for a big meeting, presentation, or proposal. And because we are responsible adults, we readily jump in to assist a rookie or a struggling salesperson facing a situation we know they are not capable of handling properly without us. And while we should take satisfaction in helping out in all of those situations, aren't these just table stakes, the bare minimum for managers?

Yes, reactive coaching is a requirement of the job. We need to be ready to jump in when needed, but the point I most desperately want you to grasp is that it is the proactive, developmental, nonurgent coaching that makes your people better and drives long-term sales success. And because proactive coaching is very often the thing we skip, avoid, or postpone because it's not pressing, and we are rarely challenged by executives about how well we are developing our people, that is exactly why the very best managers plan ahead to prioritize proactive coaching.

IT IS THE PROACTIVE, DEVELOPMENTAL, NONURGENT COACHING THAT MAKES YOUR PEOPLE BETTER AND DRIVES LONG-TERM SALES SUCCESS.

PROTECTING YOUR CALENDAR TO PRIORITIZE PEOPLE DEVELOPMENT

Let's talk calendars. We touched on this briefly in chapter 2, but let's get even more practical here. The most effective and productive executives, managers, and individual contributors (salespeople) deploy the simplest of techniques to ensure the right amount of time is spent on the highest-payoff activities. They time block their calendars.

Time blocking is not only simple, it is one of the most widely accepted productivity principles on the planet. Everyone understands it, and almost everybody agrees with the concept. Yet surprisingly, very few actually deploy it!

After significant personal study on the topic of productivity, here's my fancy definition: *time blocking is the discipline of making appointments with yourself to work on your highest-payoff activities.* Said more simply, it means that we get to our calendar first before other jokers fill it up with less valuable tasks, or we get distracted with the fire du jour, and we intentionally schedule dedicated blocks of time to work on those precious few, highest-value, nonurgent activities. Proactively investing time to observe, work alongside, coach, and debrief our sellers falls squarely into that nonurgent yet critically important category.

Similar to how the best sales hunters carve out calendar time for prospecting, we as managers must do the same regarding proactive coaching. Prospecting is rarely urgent in the moment, and as I often remind sales teams, no one defaults to prospecting and new business development mode. No one. Why not? Because there's always something easier, more attractive, and definitely more urgent to do. Prospecting doesn't call the salesperson. The salesperson has to call it. Prospecting doesn't happen by accident. If it's not intentionally put in the calendar (time blocked) then it doesn't happen. I can make the case that the same is true regarding managers and proactively coaching their people. If we don't schedule it, it will not happen.

A best practice is to plan out at least one month of coaching time blocks and, even better, a full quarter at a time. There is no rocket science here. Just start creating dedicated time blocks where you'll plug in proactive coaching sessions. Some of these sessions may be "fieldwork" where you will go out and work alongside a salesperson, or they may be sales skills or deal strategy coaching sessions. These blocks can vary in duration. Some might be a full day or more if they require travel. Others may be as brief as thirty minutes to strategize on a particular customer or deal, or just to shadow a particular salesperson. Regardless of the format or specific purpose of each particular coaching episode, the bigger point is getting them into your calendar so you are protecting that precious time to be used for this high-value activity.

It is hard to offer advice on the best cadence for how often you will proactively coach each salesperson as you rotate through your roster. Every manager's situation is different. Some lead a team of two while others may manage twelve salespeople. Some sales management roles have more of a "field general" slant while others involve more operational, branch, or retail floor oversight. Because there isn't a one-size-fits-all sales management role, there is no simple rule of thumb for the proper percentage of the calendar dedicated to coaching and working alongside our salespeople. Each situation requires discretion. But this I can offer without reservation: the most effective managers maximize time spent with their people. Very similar to how I felt years ago as a salesperson, every day out in the field seeing customers was better than any day at my desk in the office. For managers, every hour spent proactively working alongside and coaching a salesperson trumps any hour spent on anything else.

STARING INTO A SCREEN AND INTERPRETING DATA DO NOT QUALIFY AS COACHING

Yes, today we have all kinds of new powerful tools available to us. Many managers have access to more data via the click of a mouse than was even imaginable a decade ago. Companies invest zillions of dollars in fancy CRM and ERP systems, and the relatively new specialty in data analytics has created a veritable army of analysts who love nothing more than slicing and dicing immeasurable amounts of information in the hopes of uncovering useful statistical gems. As companies provide managers with more powerful dashboards along with more thorough analysis of key data points, the temptation grows to "coach" and manage our people almost exclusively with our heads down while staring at screens and spreadsheets. And when you combine this data overload with all the other corporate crap heaped onto the sales manager's desk, the temptation to "coach" through screens and emails becomes even greater.

I cannot state this any more plainly: while sophisticated systems and accurate, well-sorted data can be wonderful supplements that guide us to offer more precise coaching, we must never forget the reality that we are leading people, not robots. Analytics, and easy-access, tailored data can and may be a wonderful, powerful resource, but they will never replace what managers will observe with their own eyes and gut when working with their people.

Data, even the most accurate data, looked at in isolation does not tell the whole story. I have used this analogy in the past, and it's too appropriate to not share it again here. Managers of sports teams are on the sideline, on the bench, or in the dugout during games for a reason. They don't sit in a room with a supercomputer that analyzes statistics every minute and spews out *management reports* while the game is going on! They watch the game. They observe their people. They sense things that would never show up properly in reports. Things like attitude, commitment, and body language. Furthermore, they look at heart engagement and effort and interaction with teammates. And let's not forget that during the game they also interact with their players. They see them in action. They take note of behaviors and tendencies. They praise. They critique. They sketch out plays. They encourage. They challenge. And they also make real-time decisions, even lineup changes based on what they are observing and sensing—again, because the managers are human, and they are managing other humans.

During the 2020 World Series, along with other horrified baseball fans, I witnessed the most egregious case of management malpractice by analytics (instead of observation) in history. Even if you don't follow baseball, this true story drives home a powerful and colossal lesson. What follows is the very popular article I posted to my blog the next day:

THIS MLB MANAGER BLEW IT RELYING SOLELY ON ANALYTICS RATHER THAN HIS EYES

To the horror of baseball fans across the country, Tampa Bay Rays' manager, Kevin Cash, abruptly pulled starting pitcher, Blake Snell, out of the game after giving up a hit in the sixth inning. Up to this point in the game, Snell was beyond dominant and hadn't even thrown eighty pitches! He was executing a pitching masterpiece that was a sight to behold, and I was marveling at his performance, control, power, command, etc. So shocked (and angry) to see Tampa Bay's manager headed to the mound to replace his pitcher, I took to Twitter and instantly launched this tweet, which ended up being prophetic:

> **Mike Weinberg**
>
> @mike_weinberg
>
> I'm no professional MLB manager but if I'm the Rays, there ain't no way I'm taking out my starting pitcher for giving up one hit right there. Wow. Short leash. Huge bet the bullpen will be perfect. I don't like it.
>
> 9:22 PM · Oct 27, 2020 from Des Peres, MO · Twitter for iPhone

And that was before hearing Joe Buck (who did an outstanding job announcing the game for Fox Sports) tell the audience that Snell had completely shut down the next three batters due up for the Dodgers who collectively had zero hits in six at-bats and struck out six times against him. Honestly, no one, and I mean no one (except the Dodgers) were happy to see this pitcher removed. It's not an exaggeration to say that no one agreed this was the right move.

Why am I sharing this story and my frustration about this with you? Because just like in sales, there's been a movement in baseball recently that decisions get made by management who are far from the action, sitting in their ivory towers pouring over reams of data—even *big data.* And while old-school baseball fans love to talk data and statistics, we've seen enough evidence to declare that baseball strategy managed exclusively by *analytics* has not panned out to be the great panacea it was purported to be. Said differently, just because the data analysts can produce an indigestible volume of analytics and reports doesn't necessarily mean that's a good thing, or that managerial decisions should be made solely by what the spreadsheets conclude.

The same is even more true regarding sales management. There are more technological tools, toys, and dashboards than we know what to do with. Many execs and sales managers have become data-obsessed, living with their heads buried in CRM screens, reviewing more data than a normal brain can possibly digest. Yet, these very same sales leaders often declare that they're *too busy* to work with, observe, and coach their salespeople.

The following excerpts are from the chapter in *Sales Management. Simplified* titled "Playing CRM Desk Jockey Does Not Equate to Sales Leadership."

> It's beyond comprehension how it has become the norm today to judge a salesperson's ability solely by overanalyzing each of his deals and what percentage of opportunities advance from stage to stage in the CRM. It's as if we've decided to replace

true sales experts with quantitative mutual fund managers. Just stick the manager behind a large screen with lots and lots of data under the guise that if she stares at it long enough she'll figure out which stocks to buy . . . I mean which salespeople can sell . . .

Can you imagine a Major League Baseball team manager, even one known for his love of stats, probabilities, and sabermetrics, not sitting in the dugout during the game? Not watching players perform with his own eyes? . . . **Think about the absurdity of a sports team manager sitting in his office all day (and all night) reviewing reports and data, making lineup decisions based only on what he sees on his screens and spreadsheets.**

While I wrote that [back in 2016], it was surreal watching it play itself out on TV last week!

Of course, the Tampa Bay manager was not literally away from the team studying analytical reports during the game, but it is now widely understood that his decision . . . to prematurely take the pitcher out of the game in this situation was actually predetermined before the game even started.

The bottom line is that an awful decision was made relying solely on data analytics. What's most concerning is that just about every living, breathing human with eyes and ears watching or listening to that game (including players on both teams) would have made a different decision based on what they were personally observing at the time. . . .

Let's all learn from this baseball manager's analytics-only-driven mistake. There are times when what our gut, our eyes, or our ears are telling us is superior to what the data analysts predict or what we're seeing on a CRM screen. I'm not suggesting we ignore the data, but we certainly should blend it with our personal observations—which, of course, requires that we actually prioritize spending time alongside our team members!

I rest my case. And believing I have successfully convinced you that proactive coaching is indeed a top priority, worthy of being time blocked into your calendar, and is best accomplished in person by working alongside and observing your people doing their jobs, the logical appropriate next questions are, "How do I accomplish this, and what should proactive coaching look like?"

THE THREE SIMPLE COMPONENTS OF "FIELDWORK"

Experience shows that the majority of new sales managers are excited about the opportunity to coach their team members. This makes sense because the majority of new sales managers are typically recently promoted salespeople who excelled in the job and are chomping at the bit for the opportunity to help their salespeople increase effectiveness. But there are also new sales managers who either have never been in an individual contributor sales role or who may be assuming this new sales management position more as a matter of necessity than by choice. People in this latter group typically carry a good deal of discomfort into the role, particularly around the topic of having to coach sellers who likely know way more about sales than they do. This is completely understandable, and it's for this group of managers that I have very good news.

It is not necessary to have been a sales superstar to succeed in sales management. In fact, I can make the argument that record-setting, high-ego, super-successful sellers often have the harder adjustment moving into management. These naturally gifted rockstars often lack patience with less successful team members and are often frustrated by the fact that these *average* performers are not as talented or skilled as they are.

Therefore, if you are the new manager carrying some trepidation into the role because you are intimidated by the thought of coaching people with more sales experience or expertise than you have, here's the good news and my encouragement: you do not need to be a sales nerd like me, a technician, trainer, or expert to effectively coach your salespeople. In fact, if you think about elite professional athletes and the people who coach them, how often is that coach better at playing the sport than the athlete entrusted to their coaching? Pretty much never. Show me the Major League Baseball manager who can hit, field, or pitch better than his players. Do you think Serena Williams's or Rafael Nadal's tennis coaches could even win one game against them if they played a match on the court? What are the odds that Rory McIlroy's or Nelly Korda's swing coaches would shoot a lower golf score than the players they coach? Zero chance. Ain't gonna happen.

So, let's reduce your anxiety about being put in a position where you are expected to coach people with greater skill or proficiency than you possess and break down what I refer to as the *fieldwork* aspect of coaching into its three basic components.

1. Pregame
2. In-Game
3. Postgame

As managers, regardless of our personal level of technical sales expertise, we are all capable of helping a team member prepare for a sales interaction, which for our purposes here, we will refer to simply as the "sales call." These sales calls could be scheduled or unscheduled, take place virtually, via phone, or in person. They could be initial, early-stage (discovery) meetings, or big boardroom presentations. They could take place in any number of places from the retail selling floor to the booth on the trade show floor, at a customer's construction job site, over Zoom or Microsoft Teams, in a conference room, or at a homeowner's kitchen table. No matter the stage in the sales process or the venue, managers can play a pivotal role proactively helping to prepare a salesperson for a sales call. And because I have personally observed so many salespeople conducting lame, ineffective sales calls, I tend to be very prescriptive when coaching managers on the best practices for their pregame coaching sessions to get sellers ready for sales calls. The better and more intentional we are when helping our people prepare for sales calls, the more likely that more of that coaching will stick—and that the coached sellers will continue to prepare professionally for future meetings, even when their manager is not with them.

The second aspect of coaching is when the manager is alongside a salesperson during a sales interaction. Whether simply observing or actively participating in the sales call, this in-game coaching provides a powerful opportunity to witness our people in action, firsthand. There is no better way to evaluate a salesperson's competency than to watch them in action—selling! Again, this is something every manager is more than capable of doing regardless of the manager's own level of sales expertise.

The final aspect of fieldwork coaching is the easiest. This is where we share our observations of the sales call (if we were there) or simply debrief the sales call (if we were not there). Postgame coaching provides a unique opportunity to offer quick, candid feedback that a salesperson might not otherwise receive. It also allows us to help a seller both reflect on how they did and to strategize on next steps. Again, all managers, regardless of experience level, are capable of sharing observations and helping a salesperson think through follow-up action items and next steps.

WORKING *WITH* OUR PEOPLE CREATES A LASTING, MEANINGFUL IMPACT

If you will be so kind as to allow me one more sports analogy, I am compelled to share a truly powerful, game-changing experience on the golf course that translates perfectly to sales and sales management. In this particular case, I was the student who benefited tremendously from a perfectly executed episode of in-field coaching, and this story will motivate you to maximize the time spent working alongside your people.

Previously I mentioned my newfound passion for golf and obsession with improving my game. For most of my adult life I have avoided hobbies. Raising three active children and joyfully chauffeuring them to and attending their activities, along with juggling my own travel and workload, did not leave much calendar bandwidth available for hobbies. That changed back in the spring of 2020 when we were all locked down as the COVID-19 pandemic raged. My youngest son, Kurt, who loves golf, was home with us after his university went completely virtual midsemester. Like everyone else, we were bored, and since one of the few activities you could actually do during the lockdown was play golf, Kurt and I began to play. And play we did!

To say I caught the golf bug would be an understatement. Videos on YouTube. Countless trips to the driving range.

Exploring various public courses before joining a golf club. Getting fitted for new clubs. Most important of all, finally engaging a coach for lessons. And not just any old coach. I had an unfair advantage in selecting a golf instructor. I'm good friends with a man named Brian Fogt who also just happens to be the number one rated golf instructor in the state of Missouri. It's not a stretch to say that he did me a massive favor taking me on as a project. Without a doubt, I am his least-accomplished golf student.

After a few lessons my swing and my game showed significant improvement. For the first time, I was consistently able to start breaking 90. I was thrilled. But over the next year as my schedule heated back up and travel resumed, I stopped getting lessons and my game plateaued. Due to our schedules, Brian and I had not been able to spend any time together—either socially or on the golf range. One evening he called and asked if I had a few hours available late that coming Saturday afternoon. He asked if I would like to play nine holes of golf with him at my course and then grab dinner together. Are you kidding? Of course! I jumped at the chance although I was also a bit nervous thinking about the pressure of playing on the course in front of a true pro. I think the feelings I had were probably similar to how most salespeople feel when they know their manager is going to spend time with them observing their sales calls.

Brian was already at the practice range warming up when I arrived at my club. That's what professionals do; they show up early. Within one minute of greeting him I realized how similar this felt to a salesperson meeting up with a manager to work together, and my antennae went up as I began dual processing this in-field coaching experience through both sales and golf lenses. What transpired that late Saturday afternoon not only transformed my golf game, but it gave me a fresh appreciation for the power of coaching and fieldwork. So much so, that afterward I went home and immediately sketched out a blog post titled "If Sales Managers Would Do for Their People What My Golf Coach Just Did for Me!" and later turned the story into a podcast episode, because so many people were asking for more details about this transformative experience.

1. PREGAME COACHING

After exchanging a few minutes of small talk and pleasantries, Brian pivoted to business, and his demeanor became more serious. As you follow along with the progression of this story, note how intentional he was about every aspect of this "fieldwork" coaching session.

He started by inquiring about my recent play and wanted to know which areas of my game were stronger and which needed work. Then he asked me what my objectives were for our round together. Obviously, I could not help but immediately relate this to the manager preparing for a sales call with a salesperson asking, "What is a win for us today? What are we trying to walk away with from this customer/prospect meeting? What's our big objective?" My mind began exploding from all the combined golf and sales management goodness taking place!

Concerned with more than just mentally preparing his student for the round, coach Brian also wanted to ensure that I had the tools necessary to accomplish my mission. While I was hitting warm-up shots on the range, he perused the clubs in my bag and pulled out my relatively new putter. After taking a few practice strokes with the putter himself, he asked what I thought about it, to which I replied that I loved the look and alignment line, but it felt a bit light. He agreed with my assessment and then reached into one of the dozen pockets in his gigantic professional-size golf bag and pulled out a roll of lead tape. "Mike, you keep working on your irons while I add some weight to this putter head."

Brian multitasked, keeping one eye on my warm-up while adding strip after strip of lead tape to the bottom of my putter. Once he was convinced I had spent enough time warming up my long game, Brian directed me over to the practice putting green so I could get the feel for using this now much heavier putter. He had me practice different length putts, offered a few tips, and then we walked into the customer's office, I mean, over to the first tee box to begin our round.

2. IN-GAME COACHING

Even though I had probably played this hole (and this course) fifty times, Brian stopped me before I teed up the ball. "Mike, what's your approach to this fairway? Where is your desired landing area for your drive, and what will that leave you to the green for your second shot?" I did not impress him with my vague response, so he continued his questioning. "It feels windier than normal today. How is that going to affect your club selection and ball flight? What's the smartest shot we can play here that maximizes your chance to hit the green in two?" Again, not super excited about my answer, Brian began talking me through my options and also shared his perspective on the best way to attack the hole.

My first-time sales manager friend, let's pause the story here and reflect for a moment.

I had not even put the first ball in play but already received more valuable coaching than I could've imagined. Look again at Brian's intentionality. He was laser focused on preparing me to play my absolute best. Nothing was taken for granted—not my mental state, objectives for the round, equipment, warm-up, or strategy for playing the first hole. As this was happening in real time, my mind vacillated back and forth from the amazing benefit I was receiving from this intentional, *proactive* coaching, to the sad reality that so few sales managers take their coaching responsibility anywhere close to as seriously as Brian took his. The contrast was striking, and I could not stop asking myself this question: How much better equipped, prepared, and effective would salespeople be if their managers would do for them what my golf coach was doing for me?

As helpful and productive as the pregame coaching was, the best was yet to come. The next ninety minutes actually playing the course with my coach in tow were game altering. I was playing my pretty typical round of golf. Some good shots. Some average shots. Some pathetic shots. And Brian, being the consummate professional, was careful not to say too much or put too many thoughts in my head. There were times I could tell that he wanted to offer more preshot advice or postshot analysis, but he restrained himself for my sake knowing that an amateur can only handle so much information and feedback at one time. But on the fifth hole I got into trouble and found myself in a dangerous situation. It's a short downhill par three with a large pond surrounding the front and right side of the green. Overcompensating to avoid the water, I swung too hard and hit the ball a bit thin. The poor strike resulted in an ugly, screaming, low line drive that flew twenty yards over the green, leaving a very difficult pitch shot back uphill to the green. The ball had nestled down in the rough, and if I overcooked the pitch, it would run through the green into the water hazard on the other side, but if I wimped out and didn't have enough club head speed, I'd never get it high enough to get back onto the green.

Aware that I was frustrated and a bit intimidated by the challenge before me, Brian wandered over to assess the situation, calm me down, and help me think through my options. I loved how he asked thought-provoking questions that forced me to think on my own before he offered suggestions for approaching the shot. "Mike, based on this lie, which of your wedges is the best choice? Where do you need to land this ball to give yourself a putt for par?" We agreed on the best wedge and then Brian shifted from questioning coach to instructing coach. He pointed to an exact spot on the edge of the green about twenty-five yards from the ball. "Mike, I want you to land the ball right here." I took a few practice swings and then with firmness he said, "You got this. Land it right here." Shockingly, I executed the tough shot as planned, landed it pretty darn close to the spot he had selected, and it trickled to within ten feet of the hole. I still remember the feeling of amazement that I was about to putt for par (three) when I knew darn well that if I were on my own in that situation, I would probably be heading for a five or six on the hole!

As I was lining up the putt, I asked Brian to help me read the break. I said it feels like it's left-to-right, maybe three balls outside to the left. Brian walked around to view it from a couple angles and replied with a somewhat stern voice, "It's just barely left-to-right. Aim it so that half the ball is outside the cup on the left and the other half of the ball just inside the left edge." I looked at him with amusement because I'm not exactly a surgeon with the putter in my hands, so I was never that specific when reading a putt on my own. But as I reflect back on it now (and back on all the questions he asked that day), I understand that he was trying to help me narrow my focus and teach me the importance of specificity when preparing to execute. Again, what an example for us as sales managers coaching our people! And in case you are wondering, yes, I made the putt and smiled, walking away with a three on that hole, 100 percent due to the coaching received.

3. POSTGAME FEEDBACK, COACHING, AND ENVISIONING

After the nine holes we headed out in separate cars to a favorite burger joint. The entire drive I talked to myself while still dual processing the powerful experience as my mind raced back and forth from thrilled golf student to amazed sales and sales management coach. I could barely keep up with my thoughts and couldn't wait to start recapping this experience on paper. Little did I know the transformative last bit of coaching that was still to come!

While waiting for our food, Brian pulled out the scorecard and started to debrief my round. He very specifically pointed out some of my best shots of the day. He mentioned how much better I was "holding off" and keeping my hands ahead of the clubhead—something we had worked on in previous lessons. We relived that crazy fifth hole and celebrated the amazing recovery pitch and the putt I sank for par, due in no small part to his very specific coaching. But it wasn't all praise and giggles. He also addressed my worst meltdown of the day when I put up a "snowman" (eight) on a par four due to a combination of poor course management, poor preshot prep, and poor execution. It was too good of a teaching opportunity to let pass, and he wanted to make darn sure I knew exactly why I flunked that hole so I wouldn't make the same mistakes again.

Then to conclude his coaching, Brian did something so powerful, meaningful, and memorable, I'll never forget it. He took the scorecard and crossed out my score. In all caps he wrote the word *REALISTIC*. Below that he wrote in what he believed that I could (and will) begin to score on each hole in the future. He handed back the scorecard, looked me directly in the eye, and said that in a very short time I'll be shooting in the low-80s instead of 90. He encouraged me that if I kept working on the fundamentals and adopted the few things we focused on that day, I would experience a breakthrough.

It is hard to even express how much his encouragement and affirming words meant to me, and I had so much respect for his intentionality. It was clearly important to Brian that I leave our time together not only with improved knowledge but also with the belief that I could excel even when he was not with me.

The very next day, I was back at my club playing eighteen holes with some friends. I had a totally different attitude approaching the course and much higher expectations and confidence after Brian envisioning me about the golfer I was becoming the prior evening. I also prepared better before the round, asked myself smarter questions before each shot, and narrowed my focus and my aimpoint before striking the ball. I birdied the first hole and went on to shoot an 85, blowing away my previous best round at this course by four strokes! Do you think it was coincidence this record round happened after spending a few hours *with* my coach? Neither do I.

Fellow sales manager, we must get *with* our people. Aside from holding team members accountable, there is *nothing* more important we can do than helping them get better at their jobs.

BONUS RESOURCE

Download a Precall Planning Checklist at

mikeweinberg.com/thefirsttimemanager

5

BAD THINGS HAPPEN WHEN YOU ATTEMPT TO DO YOUR SALESPEOPLE'S JOBS

WE ESTABLISHED BACK IN CHAPTER 2 that the goal of sales managers is to win through their people. Often, and particularly for newer managers, this is easier said than done.

Over the past decade I have been privileged to do sales leadership consulting and training on five different continents across a variety of industries and company sizes. One of the most prevalent and problematic issues I encounter is sales managers attempting to do their people's jobs, not just occasionally but as the norm. It's a problem of epidemic proportion and seems to be a universal challenge regardless of geography, industry, or company size.

So many sales managers are operating in what I call "hero mode." Their default is to *do* rather than to lead, coach, or hold accountable. It's understandable. There are common reasons why managers play sales team hero, and we'll examine those shortly, but before I hold up a mirror to help you see which of these causes may be leading you astray (or will tempt you in the future), let me start the introspection with some simple questions:

- Are you feeling overwhelmed at work and that there are often not enough hours in the day to get it all done?
- Do you sometimes feel like you are carrying the weight of your entire team and that if you are not there (for the prep session, the customer meeting, the proposal, the __________) that it won't get done well or done at all?
- Have you had the thought recently that you feel like you are doing five people's jobs instead of one job?

If you answered yes to any or all of those, it is possible that you are suffering some of the consequences from playing sales team hero instead of being focused on making heroes of your people. As we dive into this topic, here are two more questions to consider:

- Are you attempting to do your salespeople's jobs for them?
- Have you been doing instead of leading? Doing instead of coaching? Doing instead of holding them accountable?

I understand that it might not even be your fault that this may be happening. It is certainly conceivable that the senior leaders in your company have lost sight of the sales manager's primary responsibilities and therefore bury you in more crap than you can imagine, even if they're well intentioned. This happens all the time. But my experience reveals that, more than likely, it is the sales managers themselves continually defaulting to hero mode that creates the feeling of overwhelm and exhaustion. Said more simply, the reason so many managers are overwhelmed and *feeling* like they are doing everyone's job is because they *are* attempting to do everyone's job!

THE REASON SO MANY MANAGERS ARE OVERWHELMED AND *FEELING* LIKE THEY ARE DOING EVERYONE'S JOB IS BECAUSE THEY *ARE* ATTEMPTING TO DO EVERYONE'S JOB!

POTENTIAL CAUSES FOR SALES MANAGERS PLAYING TEAM HERO

After extensively observing managers who struggle with playing team hero instead of focusing on making their team members into heroes, I've identified six common causes. Please read through these causes slowly. And then read through them again! I'm asking you to put down your defense shields. Check your ego (particularly before seeing cause number one below). The goal here is to help you identify why you may be doing this now or may be prone to do it later.

Which of these six common causes may be contributing to you defaulting to hero mode:

1. OVERSIZED EGO

This may be the most difficult one to admit, but it sure is common, particularly among recently promoted managers. Top-performing salespeople get a lot of attention and typically enjoy significant public recognition. They see their names at the top of the sales report. They win awards. They make "Club." They tend to get a lot of attention and adoration. And while all of that is wonderful, it also tends to inflate one's ego.

Top sales performers with large egos who enjoy the limelight don't do much damage. A sales rep's self-aggrandizement and desire for praise is, for the most part, harmless. But everything changes when that same high-ego, glory-seeking individual contributor becomes the leader of a team and struggles to subdue their ego. Instead of getting satisfaction from people on their team receiving praise and adoration and attention, they crave it for themselves.

Regardless of tenure, managers who elevate themselves and self-promote to satiate their oversized egos not only demotivate their people, but they also often destroy the culture on their team. It's never healthy when the manager takes, rather than deflects, the credit.

Is it possible that you insert yourself into every situation and are compelled to put your fingerprints on every little thing your people do because you think too highly of yourself or desperately crave the credit and the limelight?

2. INTENSE PRESSURE TO DELIVER NUMBERS

Some managers quickly default to hero mode because they are ultracompetitive, love to win, hate to lose, and will do whatever it takes to hit the number. And honestly, that's a wonderful trait. Who doesn't want a leader that is hell-bent on winning? The problem, however, is that this whatever-it-takes mentality often translates into inserting themselves into the center of the action where they find themselves doing instead of coaching.

This drive and desire to win is another trait that we love to see in salespeople. Sales superstars will do whatever is necessary to win. Long hours? No problem. Go the extra mile? They'll go two miles. Jump in and cover for someone else who's not carrying their weight? Of course. But this mentality is not sustainable in a management role. It is not physically possible to jump in and cover for everyone. There simply are not enough hours in the day. If you as the manager have to be involved in every prep session, presentation, or meaningful conversation, how on earth is that realistically ever going to work?

I recognize that you are very likely more driven and more talented than the average person on your team. That's why you got the management job. But being more willing or more capable is not a free pass or excuse to play surrogate sales star, even if that is what feels natural to you. Often, it is your desire to win big or the pressure you feel or place on yourself that pushes you into whatever-it-takes hero mode.

Are you possibly using your passion to win (or the pressure on you from above) as a very convenient excuse for why you feel compelled to jump into or take over situations that would likely work out just fine without your micro involvement?

3. YOUR COMPANY'S LEGACY CULTURE PROMOTES MANAGER-AS-HERO BEHAVIOR

This is probably the simplest cause for managers playing hero. They do it because they are told to do it! It's the way their company operates. Managers are positioned as the team superhero.

I worked with one large technology company whose legacy mentality was that sales managers were supposed to be in every important meeting. If it was the last day of the quarter, the sales managers were encouraged to be on multiple airplanes and personally involved in closing as many deals as possible. I kid you not. In that organization managers were not only praised for doing their people's jobs, they were encouraged to.

Is it possible that you default to playing the hero because that is what has been implicitly modeled for you or explicitly commanded to you?

4. YOU ARE A CONTROL-FREAK MICROMANAGER

This one may be the most difficult to acknowledge. For many people, it's easy to admit and laugh about maintaining a slightly oversized ego. That is not always the case, however, when it comes to opening up about our perfectionistic, control-freak tendencies!

I won't ask you to publicly confess this, but some of you reading (or listening to) this need to at least come clean with yourselves and admit that you are indeed an anal-retentive, uptight perfectionist. And while your very high standards are admirable, your desire for perfection and your inability to leave well enough alone does damage—to yourself and to those whom you lead.

Micromanagement is the death knell to a healthy sales culture and one of the things that drives away top talent. Remember what I shared earlier about why I (and almost all successful salespeople) love sales? Freedom. No one who is good at sales enjoys having their boss do their job for them or overinstructing them on every minute detail of how it should be done. Yuck.

Friend, is it possible that you are exhausted at work and possibly damaging your personal life, too, because you refuse to let go, and your control-freak, team hero approach is creating an endless amount of work for you?

5. IT'S MORE EXPEDIENT TO DO THAN TO DEVELOP

This cause is the reverse of the last one; it's easy to admit, but harder to spot. In other words, no one ever really feels bad about doing someone else's job, and in sales, it often seems natural for the manager to jump in and save the day (or the deal). There's no shame when you *do* instead of *develop*. In fact, often there is even praise for the manager who is ensuring the salesperson's success. (Shortly I will share a brutal true story that perfectly illustrates that reality.)

We all understand that it is typically easier and faster to do something ourselves. It certainly is more expedient to catch someone a fish as opposed to coaching and mentoring them into becoming a proficient fisherman. And that's exactly why so many managers default to doing instead of leading or coaching. In most cases it's faster just to grab the fishing pole and say, "I've got this."

This is also the reason that a good percentage of sales managers have a really hard time allowing their salespeople to fully conduct joint sales calls. Often, when the manager attends a prospect or customer meeting alongside their salesperson, the manager is quick to jump in and take control as soon as they sense the salesperson struggling, even slightly. Rather than allowing the salesperson to stumble, bumble, and sweat a little, they quickly yank the wheel away and take control. While it's understandable that they want to salvage the meeting/opportunity, this hero tendency cheats the manager and the salesperson of a tremendous teaching/learning moment. I can make the argument that sometimes the value of letting the salesperson struggle, or even fail, is greater than the temporary value from rescuing that particular meeting.

Is it possible that you default to playing hero because it's easier than the heavy lifting involved to properly develop your people?

6. COVERING FOR A TALENT DEFICIENCY ON YOUR TEAM

This particular cause is brutal not only because it exists in just about every sales organization but because it creates the untenable, unsustainable never-ending cycle in which the manager must continue to operate as the hero.

Very often managers knowingly play hero because they have a talent deficiency on their sales team. They are well aware that there are people in sales roles who are unable to successfully do the required job. But instead of doing the proper, mature management thing (addressing underperformance, coaching struggling salespeople up or out, and then recruiting and training up their replacements), these managers make the conscious decision to live with insufficient talent.

This shortsighted decision to leave people in the role who cannot succeed on their own pays temporary dividends. Managers who adopt this approach temporarily save themselves the grief of having to recruit, onboard, and spool up new talent. But they then find themselves trapped in what feels like a permanent cycle of having to jump in and cover for this deficient talent. So instead of actually solving the problem, they lock themselves into having to play hero for the long term, forced to actually *sell* for and serve as the crutch for people who cannot carry their own weight.

I strongly encourage you to review the list shared previously again and take time to process these common causes that lead managers to play the team hero. Even if as a newer manager you have not yet found yourself jumping in to do rather than lead, coach, and hold accountable, I promise that in the very near future you will likely be tempted by at least one of these. And once you start playing the hero, it's exceedingly difficult to extricate yourself from that approach.

REGARDLESS OF THE CAUSE, MANAGERS WHO PLAY TEAM HERO EXPERIENCE AWFUL CONSEQUENCES

The ugly reality is that regardless of why managers play the hero, the resulting consequences are brutal, both in the short and longer term:

SHORT TERM	LONG TERM
Exhausted managers	Culture killer
Codependent salespeople	Drives away top talent
Stunted development	Manager burnout
Kills salesperson's credibility	Neither scalable nor sustainable
Sends wrong message to team	Traps the manager in hero mode
Manager becomes the bottleneck	Manager becomes unpromotable

Before unpacking a few of these awful consequences, I will make this admission: there is one positive to the manager playing hero not listed previously, although this benefit has a limited lifespan. In the very short term, the manager can possibly drive more results operating in hero mode, particularly if there is a talent shortfall on the team. But that is the *only* benefit, and it is worth repeating that it is short-lived. Every. Other. Consequence. Is. Bad.

Let's start with the obvious. It's exhausting when instead of trying to do our own job well we operate constantly attempting to do our people's jobs too. Not only does the hero manager live in a harried, perpetual state of overwhelm, the people entrusted to this manager's *leadership* (using the word loosely here) suffer, as well.

Salespeople working under hero managers often swing between confusion and codependence as they walk around wondering, "Am I supposed to take the initiative and take responsibility for my own work, or must I constantly seek my micromanager's input and approval?"

How in the world is a team supposed to work effectively when its members have no confidence? What good is a group of basically codependent salespeople who can't do anything without us, or they're afraid and insecure to do anything on their own because of how me might react?

Potentially even worse, hero managers prevent their salespeople from developing. Why would they seek to get any better at their job if we're going to do it for them? Plus, think about what happens when managers play the hero in front of customers. If the manager is the one conducting the meeting, the one continually answering the customer's questions, delivering the presentation, leading the negotiation, and so on, doesn't that effectively neuter the salesperson? I am having a visceral reaction right now, cringing as I recall experiencing this firsthand and hearing stories from other sellers about their overbearing, control-freak managers! This awful management behavior destroys the credibility of salespeople with their customers. When the customer views the manager as the chief salesperson and the one who makes all the decisions, they have no use for the salesperson and will want to deal only with the manager in the future.

How in the world is that supposed to work? Or scale? The salespeople basically become useless. They're like pawns. And this management style also sends a really odd message to the sales team. It screams that they're not that important and the manager is truly the center and star of the team. I'm not sure that's a message we want to send.

The final short-term consequence I want to highlight is that very often, the hero manager becomes the bottleneck. When managers intentionally put themselves at the center insisting that every little detail run through them, progress grinds to a halt. Rather than multiplying themselves into their people to create scale and speed, the opposite occurs. Everyone ends up vying for the manager's attention, input, and approval, while practically nothing gets accomplished.

And if you didn't like the short-term implications of managers playing team hero, just look at what happens longer term. Not only do hero leaders destroy morale and any hope of maintaining a healthy sales culture, they also create this unsustainable, untenable situation by constructing an environment where they must remain the hero. Because people are not trusted and not being developed, managers end up trapped in a self-fulfilling, permanent hero cycle where they feel even greater pressure to continue doing everyone's job.

This vicious hero cycle drives even more damaging consequences. Good salespeople get fed up and leave. Top sales talent will not remain in that type of micromanagement environment. Why would they? Only less talented, weaker sellers stay working for a hero manager. And you can see where this leads. Exactly. Hero managers only feel more justified in playing the hero, pile even more work and pressure on themselves, and eventually burn out or collapse in defeat. As if that's not punishment enough, the final nail in the coffin is that hero managers have clearly demonstrated that they are not promotable. Living in a perpetual state of overwhelm trying to do everyone's job, confusing and demotivating the troops, and running off top talent are not exactly the hallmarks of a successful leader or someone on whom companies are looking to bestow even higher levels of leadership. Running around attempting to do your entire team's job means you are not mentoring, not developing people into future leaders, and likely not sending more of your people to the "Club."

IDENTIFY THE SPECIFIC AREAS YOU MAY DEFAULT TO HERO MODE

Two years ago I was leading a workshop for a large group of a very large company's first-line sales managers. The ballroom was packed with maybe 130 people, many of whom were not yet thirty years old. This company had a healthy sales culture, attracted high-quality candidates, and often quickly promoted successful young sellers into frontline management positions.

I have tremendous respect for the sales executives in this organization and was having a blast facilitating the session because the leaders encouraged me to push the envelope and not settle for surface-level responses. After reviewing very similar information to what has been shared thus far in this chapter, I gave participants some quiet time to work through the following self-reflection exercise. I encourage you to carve out some time now for self-reflection as well:

As the sales team leader, reflect on the various areas and aspects of your job listed below while asking yourself where/how you may be operating and positioning yourself as the hero instead of the hero maker?

- Your sales management mindset and view of your role
- Your words when addressing the team or individual salespeople
- Your calendar (and how you decide who and what gets your attention)
- How you prep sales team members for sales calls/customer meetings/presentations

- The role you play during sales calls and presentations or while crafting important proposals
- How you approach coaching team members when strategizing on sales opportunities
- How your people would describe your management style
- How you report the sales team's results to the rest of your organization

In which areas did you find yourself "doing" instead of coaching or leading?

Where are you "dictating"—telling your people what to do and how to do it—instead of mentoring and "multiplying" yourself into others?

List specific examples of how and when you have been playing hero and the respective consequences resulting from that decision/approach.

I so badly wish we were in a room together so I could hear your insights and takeaways after reflecting on the various areas of your job outlined previously. Based on my experience leading sessions with newer managers, I'm quite confident you were able to identify at least one area, and more likely a handful, where you tend to default to playing hero instead of focusing on making heroes.

LET THIS HERO HORROR STORY SERVE AS A POWERFUL REMINDER

After giving this large gathering of managers plenty of time to reflect on the list, I encouraged them to *confess their hero sins* to colleagues seated around them. As is often the case during table discussion, the room got very loud, and there was plenty of laughter and finger-pointing going on at the round tables around the room.

At one table in the very back, however, I noticed participants listening intently to a young woman. Their faces were serious, and no one was laughing. I watched from afar as this one manager spoke for several minutes, obviously sharing something meaningful with her tablemates.

When it was time to wrap-up the group discussion, I grabbed the microphone and asked people to raise their hand if someone at their table shared a meaningful observation or confession about playing hero. A smattering of hands went up around the room, but as I glanced back to where the woman had everyone's rapt attention, every hand was raised. I stared in that direction long enough to get the entire room's attention, motioned with my hand, and asked simply, "Would someone like to share?"

Every person at the table pointed at the young woman, saying in unison, "Meredith does!" Meredith (not her actual name) stood up as one of the vice presidents ran a handheld mic over to her. With her voice quaking, she began to relay the story she had just shared at her table.

"I love this company and I was so thankful to be promoted and for the chance to lead a team that as a new manager last year I was committed to doing whatever was necessary for the people on my team to succeed. And succeed we did. We not only surpassed our sales goal, two individuals on my team made President's Club."

The room fell completely silent—and confused—anticipating what could be coming next and wondering where this story was going. Meredith paused to gather her composure and continued speaking at barely a whisper, "This year I had to terminate both of those people." She paused again with 130 sets of eyeballs and ears focused squarely on her.

"You see, I was overzealous as a new manager. I was committed to doing *whatever* was necessary to win and prove that I belonged in the job. So I inserted myself into every sales opportunity I could and, being completely honest with the benefit of hindsight, I am the one who 'won' President's Club for those two reps. I sold for them. I did their jobs—very well, I might add." Meredith smiled and let out an amused, relieved sigh. Everyone exhaled, a few people chuckled, affirming her transparency, and the tension started to leave the room.

She continued. "This year I matured, and came to my senses realizing that it wasn't possible to keep 'managing' the way I did as a rookie manager. I stopped joining every possible sales call and tried to be more of a coach, but it didn't take long to realize that these two reps whom *I sent* to Club were in trouble. Actually, I was the one in trouble because once I took my hands off the wheel it became obvious that these reps were neither coachable nor capable of selling on their own. I did what I could to coach them up, but it didn't work. Both ended up on performance improvement plans, and I stand before you today as likely the first sales manager in history who had to fire two sales reps who went to Club the prior year."

My first-time manager friend, whether it's from zealous young Meredith's painful public confession, or from the sixty-year-old veteran sales manager who, in a state of exhaustion and desperation on the edge of total burnout, cried out in a session that he couldn't do it anymore and just wanted his life back, I urge you with all of my being to grasp this lesson now. Regardless of circumstances, you cannot win the long-term sales management game playing the hero of your team. It is neither scalable nor sustainable. At best, it's a very short-term fix. It will kill your culture, your career, and your quality of life.

Before moving on to tackle the critical elements of smart sales-talent management in the next few chapters, please take some time to again review the causes and consequences of defaulting to hero mode and reflect on the areas of your job where this deadly approach manifests itself (or may in the future).

Maximum joy, job satisfaction, sales results, and long-term success go to the managers who learn how to win through their people!

BONUS RESOURCE

You can download the Sales Leader: Hero or Hero-Maker Assessment from mikeweinberg.com/thefirsttimemanager

6

YOUR JOB IS MUCH EASIER WITH THE RIGHT PEOPLE ON YOUR TEAM!

THERE IS NO WAY AROUND THIS SIMPLE TRUTH: to win big as a sales manager you must get the right people on your team, keep your best sellers and maximize their performance, and quickly coach up or coach out underperformers. In this chapter we begin our smart sales-talent management journey by helping to ensure that you attract the right salespeople and repel the wrong ones.

I'm not sure there is a more mysterious or challenging sales management topic than selecting talent. Every time I lead a workshop or Q and A session with sales leaders, there are myriad questions around recruiting and interviewing. Frankly, it is easy to understand the confusion because I am constantly confused by what I observe:

- Fuzzy, flowery job descriptions that do the opposite of what we'd hope

- Human resources and talent acquisition departments who appear to be clueless about the attributes of top-performing salespeople
- Casual interviews in public settings like a Panera Bread café
- Managers who dominate interviews by speaking 70 percent of the time and coming across like they're pitching their company instead of probing into the candidate's preferences, proficiencies, and past performance
- Failing to create an interview environment that allows the hiring manager to determine whether the candidate can truly sell

Based on the list above, it's no surprise that frustrated, confused managers are continually seeking help and perspective around hiring best practices.

THERE IS NO MORE CRITICAL SALES MANAGEMENT DECISION THAN *WHO* YOU ADD TO YOUR TEAM!

Before getting granular about conducting great interviews, it's important that we dispel a few myths about sales talent and also review what I have dubbed the "Two Iron Laws of Recruiting."

THE FALLACY OF THE HIGHLY RELATIONAL, COLLABORATIVE SALES SUPERSTAR

I am fully aware that you may consider writing me off as a heretic after reading this. And while the old adage that "people buy from people they like" is at least partially true, what follows needs to be said as plainly as possible. The very best salespeople exhibit these two characteristics:

- They are intensely competitive
- They are not conflict averse (meaning they don't shy away from a fight)

So while the kindhearted harmonizers in your HR department like to write warm, fuzzy job descriptions strongly encouraging you to bring gentle, agreeable, highly relational team players and collaborators onto your sales team, I vehemently disagree and offer a contrarian perspective. Since the very best salespeople on planet Earth, regardless of their specific role (meaning both hunters and account managers charged with maintaining and growing revenue within existing accounts) are highly competitive and not fearful of conflict, shouldn't we be looking for candidates who are sales killers instead of collaborators?

Do not read more into this than I'm actually writing. In no way am I suggesting you recruit unlikable jerks, prima donnas, and difficult people. But I am emphatically making the case that if we are going to win as sales managers then we need to staff up with people who exhibit the characteristics of sales winners. And very often, the ultracompetitive people who are willing to advocate for the companies/solutions they represent (and for themselves), and who push through resistance when prospecting, bust objections, dislodge incumbents, secure next steps, follow up intently, confidently sell at full price, ask for and close deals . . . these people don't necessarily look, smell, or feel like the collaborator candidates your HR people fantasize about in their flowery job descriptions.

Again, these winning sales attributes don't apply only to salespeople in hunting roles. The highest-performing territory or account managers see themselves as much more than glorified customer service reps. They are not just pacifists and territory peacekeepers who placate and babysit customers, play parts delivery person, or order taker. The very best account managers actually *sell*. They are proactive. They *penetrate* into accounts, create new and expand existing relationships, and Pac-Man their way through customers, gobbling up as much new business as possible. And while these top-producing account/territory managers may indeed be likable and highly relational, above all, they keep score, play to win, and are unafraid to pursue new business.

So be wary of those who may not understand sales when they pontificate to you about who the best candidates are for your team. I guarantee you, sales manager, that if your team doesn't deliver the results, no one will applaud you or offer a free pass for underperformance because you built the most relational, likable team.

THE TWO IRON LAWS OF RECRUITING

Managers who are serious about building winning cultures and winning teams get serious about recruiting. From my years observing leaders who do this well and those who don't, I have drafted what I refer to as the Two Iron Laws of Recruiting:

IRON LAW 1: Recruit ahead of the need

The secret to becoming a highly successful recruiter is recruiting ahead of the need. Imagine how much faster and easier it would be to fill a job opening if there were a *bench* of potential new-hire candidates that you had already been grooming.

I've spent significant time working with highly successful search firms—both as a coach to and a client of several firms.

One of the reasons they are so successful placing the perfect candidates? They. Recruit. Ahead. Of. The. Need. When these top-notch recruiters secure a new search, they are not starting from scratch. They tap into the network of passive jobseekers that they've already been cultivating and very often have a handful of potentially ideal candidates lined up to consider for their client's open position.

Similarly, sales managers who make recruiting a priority, who dare to block time for recruiting ahead of the need, even when they don't have a current opening, these managers are the ones best positioned to land the best candidate! The challenge, akin to our earlier discussion about how proactive coaching of our people is critically important but rarely urgent, is that most managers are so busy simply trying to survive the daily grind that they have difficulty rationalizing the value of blocking time to recruit when there isn't an imminent need.

The title of this chapter is not a false promise. If you want to make your job easier and you are serious about building a winning team, you must carve out time, even if it's just a few hours per month, for proactive recruiting. How? Build your referral network. Talk to customers. Reach out to suppliers. Cultivate a referring culture within your own organization by regularly reminding associates at your company that you are perpetually interested in being introduced to potential candidates for sales roles. Troll LinkedIn. Connect with competitors' salespeople.

It's okay to post a job description and start meeting candidates even if you may not have an open position. Yes, I just said that. And it's not only permissible but a best practice to schedule calls or coffees with people whom you feel are potentially attractive candidates even if you don't have an imminent need (current opening to fill).

I know this concept may sound crazy, but let me ask . . . if you just happened to meet the *perfect candidate*, and I mean perfect, someone you'd regret for years not making a spot for on your team, wouldn't you do *everything* in your power to find or create a position for this ideal hire? I would, even if I had to beg, borrow, and steal (from somewhere else in the budget)!

There's another added benefit from continually recruiting ahead of the need. It bolsters our high-performance culture, sending the clear message to everyone on and around our team that we are serious about winning, that we are *open for business* and always on the lookout for top talent to enhance or upgrade our team. And although not a primary motivation for continually recruiting, this approach to talent management also keeps underperformers on their toes. They become keenly aware that we are building a high-performance team and everyone on the team must earn their spot in the lineup.

IRON LAW 2: Never, ever hire a candidate who is not better than the average on your team

The second iron law of recruiting is as simple as it gets and safeguards managers from doing what is expedient instead of what is right. We never, ever hire a candidate who is not better than the average on the team.

This is a nonnegotiable tenet of smart talent management. Let me put it even more plainly because violating law 2 puts us on a dangerous, slippery slope from which it is almost impossible to recover: *If the candidate does not raise the bar (the average talent level), then walk away.*

I know what you're thinking because I've heard it time and time again. "Come on, Mike. You don't understand. I have holes in my team that must be filled. I'm dying just trying to do my own job while (poorly) attempting to cover for, and pick up the slack created by, these open positions. And that's before you factor in how much time is sucked up with recruiting and interviewing. I'm not saying that I'll settle for a warm body or someone who can fog a mirror, but it is hard to find good talent, and it looks like I'm going to be making offers to candidates whose talent level is significantly below my average team member."

Again, I hear you, and I understand, but I am asking you to play out this "just settle" approach with me. What will immediately happen when you start bringing people, even one person, onto your team who actually *lowers the bar*? Think about it for a moment. What message are you sending to existing team members? The split second your team concludes that you settled, that you, their leader, threw in the towel and hired a new teammate that doesn't really belong on the same field with them, what did you just do to your (supposedly) "high-performance culture?"

When tackling this topic during workshops, I often quote a brilliant leadership consultant and talent guru with whom I've worked. David Kuenzle would regularly remind executives (me included) that regardless of how urgent the mission to grow the organization or fill critical empty positions, "Very often, no breath is better than bad breath." And David would regularly remind me that his point was doubly true when looking to add sales talent. As painful as an open slot may be, in the long run, we are always better off waiting until we find the right person than simply filling the role to relieve our short-term problem.

Let me mention, however, one exception. Law 2 does not apply when adding a "rookie" to your team. While we still certainly want the highest-caliber rookie, if you are seeking to add a recent college graduate or someone with limited or no sales experience and no track record, that new hire obviously will not raise the bar for your team. Personally, I love hiring people without sales experience and enjoy the process of mentoring them into professional sellers. There is nothing better than when one of these sales newbies blossoms into a sales superstar. So, please, don't let law 2 dissuade you from bringing inexperienced candidates onto your team.

THREE MAJOR MISTAKES THAT SABOTAGE SALES INTERVIEWS

Once we are clear about the characteristics desired in our ideal hire, committed to recruiting ahead of the need, and never, ever settling on a candidate that fails to raise the bar, it is time to upgrade our interviews.

I observe three common interviewing mistakes that hurt hiring managers' ability to sort out the wheat from the chaff, or the champs from the chumps, and make great hiring decisions:

TALKING TOO MUCH

Similar to how salespeople should be speaking less than they're listening to prospects during sales calls, managers need to stop talking so much during interviews. We want the salesperson on the hot seat. We need the *salesperson* (the candidate) to be speaking the vast majority of the words. So we need to be careful that we're not blabbing away, turning the interview into a pitch where we're trying to impress the candidate with *our* greatness while overpromoting our company and its culture. The true purpose of the interview (that we often forget) is to find out whether this candidate can sell, not for us to *sell* the candidate!

FAILING TO MAKE CANDIDATES SELL THEMSELVES

The second common mistake is that we never really uncover whether candidates have what it takes to succeed in sales. We get a feeling for whether they can interview and whether we like them, and certain things about them, but we don't necessarily put candidates in situations that demonstrate their sales ability.

BEING TOO PREDICTABLE

Very often the interviews we conduct are predictable. Too predictable. It's as if the candidates know what's coming. They've heard our assortment of canned, overused interview questions, and they're ready with somewhat rehearsed answers. Because we are not challenging candidates with creative questioning that forces them to react in the moment, we don't learn anywhere near as much as we could from interviews.

This deadly combination of hiring managers being so predictable, talking too much, and not creating an environment that forces candidates to demonstrates their sales ability produces ineffective interviews. So ineffective that we often get duped . . . duped into hiring candidates that we may like but honestly have no clue whether they will succeed at the job.

Before diving into my favorite sales interview questions, let's pause for just a moment to expand on the concept of likability. Earlier in the chapter I gave you the opportunity to declare me a heretic for making light of the likability factor. It's not that being likable isn't important; it is. But likability, in and of itself, is not a driver of sales success. I've met many, many highly likable salespeople who lived at the very bottom of the sales rankings. I've had the unpleasurable experience of having to fire several not just likable but lovable salespeople. There's almost nothing worse in business than having to terminate a wonderful human being because they simply were not a fit for the role.

The harsh reality is that Sales. Is. About. Results. Likability, without other key factors, does not necessarily translate into significant success in sales.

I know this sounds obvious, but our most important mission when selecting a candidate is to gain an understanding whether this person can sell. And the very best way to accomplish that is to see how the candidate behaves in a sales environment. Therefore, our job is to make the interview resemble a sales conversation (sales call) as closely as possible because we want to observe our candidate's sales ability firsthand—and in this case, whether they can sell themselves! And I cannot state this any more plainly, my new sales manager friend: if your candidates cannot sell themselves to you during the interview, how in the world will they succeed selling your product/services/solution? The easiest thing in the world for salespeople to sell should be themselves. Right?

Before we examine a list of favorite, useful interview questions that truly help determine a candidate's sales efficacy, let me offer a few tips on evaluating how well your interviewee prepared for this *sales call* with you.

Professionals prepare. Therefore, from the moment we greet candidates we are looking for clues that they put significant effort into getting ready for the interview. How quickly are they demonstrating the research done before meeting with you? Did they peruse recent posts on your social channels and deploy what they learned to build rapport more easily? Did they read recent news releases from your company or learn a few meaningful things about you and the business so they could comfortably and casually weave those discoveries into the conversation? The bottom-line question is, did they put the work in similar to what we would expect them to do before going on a sales call? Or are they winging it?

My daughter, Haley, recently earned her master's degree in landscape architecture and city planning from a top national program. As her personal sales coach, it was my privilege to help prepare Haley for interviews. She scored an interview with the principal of a progressive, well-known firm that did exactly the type of inner-city work that interested her. While coaching Haley up to prepare well, I gently reminded her that her education was simply table stakes. "Haley, they know you just earned a graduate degree from a top-five program in the country for this type of architecture. They know you are as prepared as a rookie architect can be for her first job. It's other things like your desire, passion, and professionalism that will win them over in the interview." I encouraged her to search YouTube for talks the principal of this firm had recently given and invest time in other places seeing what leaders from this firm were speaking about and what mattered to them. She not only discovered a few gems but did the extra prep work, figuring out how to tie what she learned into her answers to questions during her interview. Her sales coach is smiling as he types this ☺. Isn't that exactly the kind of preparation we want our salespeople doing before meeting with customers?

Along with determining whether the candidate invested the time and energy doing appropriate research, I am also always curious to learn if they have put in the work on selling themselves. Did they practice telling their own story? Can they clearly articulate their successes they're sharing with you? Did they put the effort into crafting the bullet points in their résumé and were they able to casually weave in those success stories during the interview? Or did you have to work hard trying to get the candidate to put their best foot forward?

Lately, I've had several frustrating interviews in which candidates seemed unable to effectively articulate their successes.

That is a huge red flag. Again, if *sales* candidates have a hard time making a compelling case for themselves, how can we expect them to effectively make the case for the products and solutions we are hiring them to sell!

IF *SALES* CANDIDATES HAVE A HARD TIME MAKING A COMPELLING CASE FOR THEMSELVES, HOW CAN WE EXPECT THEM TO EFFECTIVELY MAKE THE CASE FOR THE PRODUCTS AND SOLUTIONS WE ARE HIRING THEM TO SELL!

Recently, as a favor to a friend, I took a networking meeting with a gentleman looking for a sales job. He had a decently impressive résumé, but when I asked what he was most proud of accomplishing at his last place of employment, he offered a rather mundane answer. What he shared was so lame that I squinted, shook my head, intentionally looked at him quizzically, and inquired again trying to get him to articulate one of the more impressive gems from his résumé, "Okay, and *what else* were you most proud of?" After yet another lame response, I began to get the picture as to why this person was having a tough time securing a sales job! I looked intently at my struggling new friend and then pointed to the bullet on his résumé highlighting the significant sales increase he achieved over a three-year period. I then asked with exasperation, hoping to wake him out his slumber, "Why didn't you mention this sales increase when I asked what you accomplished!"

Salespeople have to sell. They must be able to conduct a sales conversation and present their offering in an attractive, compelling way. They won't succeed just handing out brochures. And similarly, if a candidate thinks a well-written résumé is going to trump their inability to *sell you* during the interview, they are sorely mistaken.

SEVEN FAVORITE INTERVIEW QUESTIONS TO BETTER EVALUATE SALES CANDIDATES

To properly put candidates to the test, we want to create an environment with a degree of uncertainty, similar to a sales call. The questions below will help you see through the smoke screen, cut through the crap, observe how candidates think on their feet and react in a real sales situation, and help you better determine how well they can sell.

1. WHY ARE WE HERE?

I start every interview with this question: "Why are we here?" It's a total curveball that should immediately alert the candidate that this is not going to be the standard, run-of-the-mill interview. The question is intentionally vague and provides an opportunity to see how the interviewee handles a question they were not expecting.

Typically, the candidate will repeat the question back to me and then I just smile big and repeat, "Exactly. Why are we here?" And now right at the outset you get the chance to watch your candidate improvise on the spot. Depending on the response, I may ask a follow-up question to have the candidate expand on something they mentioned, or I'll just leave it at that and move ahead to my next favorite question.

2. WHAT'S YOUR DEAL?

Three simple words: "What's your deal?" I ask it just like that, and then I shut up because that's what you do when you probe, right? You let the silence build and pay close attention to what happens next. Again, the surprised candidate will often mimic back saying, "What's my deal?" Resist the urge to jump in and offer more direction because what comes next speaks volumes.

Unfortunately, candidates often (mis)interpret what I am seeking here and launch into a thorough (boring) recap of their entire career history and basically read their résumé to me. Because I'm evaluating their sales ability and paying attention to whether they are tracking with my nonverbal reaction to their long-winded, boring answer, I just let them go. And go. And go.

Part of the reason I ask this question is because my fantasy candidate will just come right out with something wonderful and compelling like: "I love sales. I'm here because I'm looking for an incredible opportunity to make a difference for my customers, my employer, and myself. It looks like the position that you are looking to fill is a perfect fit for my gifts and my experience, and I'm hoping to show you how I could bring tremendous value to your organization and why I'm the best candidate for the position."

As you might imagine, it's pretty rare that I hear that kind of answer, but I love the "what's your deal?" question because we learn a ton about the candidate. And if the question doesn't produce much useful information, particularly about the candidate's passion for sales, I then may ask, "Who has served as a valuable sales mentor?" or "Can you describe your personal philosophy of sales?" These questions set them up well for what comes next.

3. TELL ME WHY YOU LOVE SALES

This is a critical question because sales is as much or more about the heart than it is the head. I'm not interested in adding people to my team who don't love what they do. As I've written elsewhere, there may be accountants, software engineers, and project managers who do good work without being passionate about their jobs, but I've never once met a highly successful dispassionate salesperson. We cannot afford to hire someone who doesn't love sales!

So I just ask it point blank and then sit back and listen. "Tell me why you love sales." I will not interrupt the candidate, and if they pause or stumble long enough and I don't feel like they've given me enough, I will motion my head to communicate that I'm looking for more. From my perspective, if they cannot answer this question well, it's pretty much a deal breaker. If they don't really love sales and they can't talk about being competitive and results oriented and having the chance to work independently, and they're not busting with pride to talk about their past successes and why sales is in their blood, then there is a better candidate out there!

At this point, we are through the *warm-up* phase of the interview and starting to get a feel for some of the intangibles this person brings to the party and whether they handle themselves well in a potentially unfamiliar and uncomfortable situation. Now it's time to transition into the *heavy lifting* questions and learn about our candidate's past successes and how they will approach the job.

4. TELL ME ABOUT SOME OF YOUR RECENT SALES SUCCESSES AND BIGGEST WINS

This is where I make the salesperson share a whole lot about their recent successes. Obviously, this works well only with someone who has been in sales before and has had some success (which is what makes them a stronger candidate). Again, typically, when I'm hiring a salesperson, I'm not looking for a rookie, so the details of past successes are of utmost importance.

"Tell me about a few of your recent wins. I would love to hear you brag about some of your sales victories." Candidates who have a successful track record smile when getting asked this, and you can see those who don't have many top-of-mind successes start to do mental gymnastics as they figure out what the heck they are going to tell you. And while they are processing, I add this little tidbit, "And I want to hear the whole story."

Getting the full picture is particularly important when we're interviewing for a "hunter" position. We need to uncover whether this person can hunt—that they can self-generate sales opportunities and that they understand how to fill the top of the funnel. To help the candidate better understand what I'm seeking, I often reiterate that I want the whole story, all the way back to the beginning. "Tell me how you even decided to target that particular prospect, and how you *got in* there in the first place? Tell me how you pursued the prospect, how you secured the meeting, how you created the opportunity, how you met with stakeholders, did effective discovery, advanced the deal, used your resources, and then share some detail about what happened throughout the presenting, proposing, negotiating stages all the way through closing the deal."

You can see my mission here. As hiring managers, these details matter and help us separate the professional sales hunters from the poseurs. It is imperative for us to get an accurate picture of the candidate's sales acumen and ability to create, advance, and close deals. Even more importantly for hunting positions, answers to this question provide valuable insight to whether the candidate had to *create* (self-generate) sales opportunities. This is absolutely critical if we are putting someone into a position that requires them to prospect for new business. If we expect the new hire to proactively fill the top of the pipeline with new opportunities, it behooves us to ensure they have been successful doing that in the past!

Often when I ask for details about creating sales opportunities, candidates begin telling the story in the middle of the sales cycle because that is where the opportunity was handed to them or when they got involved. They did not have to prospect or self-generate the opportunity. The lead was provided by marketing or a business development rep, or an existing customer expressed a need. Often the opportunity materialized because the potential customer went out to the market searching for a new supplier or to issue a request for proposal. There is a big difference between a salesperson who is competent at *chasing* an opportunity presented to them versus the salesperson who is adept at *creating* an opportunity through their own proactive sales effort. I repeat, if you're looking for a sales hunter, I strongly suggest you clearly identify candidates' past willingness, ability, and demonstrated success in hunting.

Forcing candidates to articulate the details of recent sales success also protects managers from making an oft-repeated and deadly mistake—hiring the industry veteran dud. This common malady occurs when we hire someone who *supposedly* is, or was, a top producer at a similar business or competitor. The person *supposedly* comes ready to hit the ground running, knows the industry, and even comes with, forgive the phrase, a Rolodex of contacts and established relationships.

I cannot count the number of companies who've been fooled in this nightmare scenario. We (incorrectly) assume that just because this person was really successful once upon a time at a competitor, or somewhere in the industry, that they're going to continue to be successful. So we make an offer to the grizzled industry veteran because it seems like the safe bet and then months later wonder what in the world happened. Why is this *supposed* past superstar not bringing in sales for us? Well, what happened is that we did not ask the right questions or uncover that this industry veteran had actually "retired in place" a long time ago. The seller was a top producer at their previous company only because they were there the longest. Because of their tenure, they managed the biggest accounts. They put up big numbers simply due to seniority. It's easy to pad the score when the best customers, opportunities, and leads get handed to you! But now as your salesperson, the playing field is not tilted in their favor. Not only don't they have the biggest accounts or get handed the best leads, but you painfully discover that this expensive veteran's skills and passion have atrophied. They have lost both the desire and discipline to hunt for new business.

The "tell me the whole story" question protects hiring managers from pontificators great at talking theory, poseurs positioning themselves as hunters, and veterans who retired in place years ago. It's our job to force candidates to detail recent successes and to get the whole story from beginning to end. "Successes" is plural because we are looking for more than one. If this candidate is a winner, they should have plenty of success stories that they are excited to share. And there's nothing more exciting than when the interviewee blows you away with several compelling success stories and you realize that you very likely have found your ideal candidate.

5. WHAT WOULD YOU DO IN YOUR FIRST SIXTY DAYS?

This is one of my favorite questions because it not only reveals how well they prepped for the interview but, more importantly, provides a window into how candidates think and will approach the job. I refer to it as "The Sixty-Day Scenario" question.

Say to the candidate:

> Let's assume you get the job offer and we bring you on board. Your first week you go through a basic bare-bones orientation.

> We get your email address set up, introduce you to a few key people in the company, provide you with the obligatory company-branded quarter-zip pullover and logoed large Yeti tumbler, and your business cards.
>
> Here's what I want you to do. Play out this scenario for me. After we get you on board and through that brief orientation, then I (your sales manager) am going on a sixty-day sabbatical. I'll be unreachable for two months. What are you going to do? I want to hear how you'll approach the job in those first sixty days. Where will you start? What will you learn? How will you begin doing the job and attacking the market? What will you accomplish during those sixty days that I'm away and you are on your own independently working away? On day sixty-one when I return, you and I will meet so you can share what you've learned and what you've accomplished in your first two months.

It's telling to observe the candidate's reaction to this question. Some start to smile and salivate because you just tossed them a softball right down the middle. Other candidates squirm in discomfort and disbelief that you are actually requiring them to think out loud instead of conducting the routine, predictable interview asking them to list their strengths and weaknesses.

I truly want to pull the best, most-thoughtful response out of the candidate, so I strongly suggest that they take their time formulating the answer and even recommend they sketch out a few notes before rattling off the first few ideas that come to mind. For emphasis, I restate that I am very interested in hearing their thinking, suggest again they take their time because I care deeply about what they will share. And then I don't say another word.

What happens next speaks volumes. The immature or amateur salesperson, who wasn't listening to me coach them in the moment to be thoughtful and answer slowly, immediately starts rattling off what they're going to do. I will attempt to help them one more time by holding up my hand like a stop sign and repeating, "I am really encouraging you to think about this. Maybe sketch out some notes because I want to hear your whole plan. I am in no hurry." And if it is apparent they are stuck or stumped, I'll offer a bit of guidance suggesting they include what resources they might seek, how they will build or prioritize their customer list (or territory plan), or begin learning the company story to craft sales messaging, or find customer success stories and use cases they can deploy, and so on.

When we set up this scenario well, we learn a lot about the salesperson's experience, professionalism, and sales acumen. This sixty-day scenario question combined with the previous question forcing candidates to articulate details about their recent sales successes typically paints a very clear picture about what this person brings to the table.

6. WHAT DO YOU WISH I WOULD'VE ASKED YOU THAT I DIDN'T?

Earlier this year a client CEO of a smaller company asked me to interview a candidate who was recommended to him by a friend. The candidate didn't impress me from the get-go and his answers to my five questions left me wanting more. But I wanted to give this person the benefit of the doubt because he came rather highly recommended to my client and figured maybe he was just having an off day. Perhaps my questions weren't helping him articulate his true value/potential. So I teed up the easiest question I could think of that would allow the candidate to direct me anywhere he wanted to go. "Joe, what do you wish I would've asked you that I didn't?"

Truly, this was intended as a batting practice pitch right down the middle, hoping that Joe would absolutely crush it over the fence (because any true salesperson would launch that pitch into orbit).

I eagerly awaited Joe's response as I nodded affirmatively into the webcam hoping he'd take advantage of this wide-open last opportunity to win me over. He didn't. Joe weakly responded with, "I'm good. I think we covered everything."

Immediately, I knew that my initial gut instinct was correct and that this wasn't the right candidate. His weak answers earlier in the interview accurately portrayed him. Candidacy terminated.

Let's contrast Joe's response to this same question to one from a different candidate I recently interviewed. From the moment Mark said hello and brilliantly shared, "why he was here" and "what's his deal," I knew I was with a winner. It was pretty much love at first sight. By the time we got around to question 6 my mind was already made up; we were going to do everything possible to land this candidate. But just for fun, I tossed the softball gently down the middle, "Mark, is there anything you wished I asked you today that I didn't?" Mark hit that pitch so hard I think the ball is still circling the Earth! He replied, "Mike, I would love you to ask me about this enormous deal I won with my number one dream prospect while selling for this tiny company against giant competitors. It's a great story. Do you have time to hear it?"

Sales manager friend, by this point in the book I believe you can actually picture the smile on my face as I recount this great experience speaking with Mark. This is the type of candidate we want to add to our team—one that will *raise the bar* (Iron Law 2). Use question 6 whenever you want to give a candidate the opportunity to put their best foot forward. If they swing and miss that probably tells you all you need to know.

7. WHY DO YOU THINK YOU ARE THE BEST CANDIDATE?

I suggest saving this question for last because we don't need to ask it in every interview. It's there for the times when we are not sure a candidate has truly differentiated themselves or won us over. It provides yet one more chance for candidates to put their best foot forward. You're opening the door giving the candidate permission to freely brag. Any legitimate "A player" will understand how to handle this and should be ready to offer several compelling reasons they belong on your team.

THE BEST CANDIDATES CONCLUDE INTERVIEWS LIKE SALES PROFESSIONALS CONCLUDE SALES CALLS

While I guarantee that these seven favorite questions will upgrade your interviews and greatly increase insight into candidates, let's wrap this chapter on the importance of getting the *right people* on your team with a final reminder that the interview is indeed a sales call. In this situation, your candidate is the salesperson, and you are the prospect. So let's take advantage of the opportunity to evaluate how well this candidate can sell by observing how adept they are at concluding the conversation (sales call).

As someone who coaches salespeople on how to conduct professional, consultative sales calls, there are things that I'm looking for a salesperson to do near the end of the meeting. Most notably, I am looking to see if they attempt to flesh out potential objections and then try to secure some kind of commitment for the next step while also professionally *asking for the business.*

When it's obvious we're getting near the conclusion of the interview, I'll often pause awkwardly and fumble around intentionally to indicate we are almost done because I'm looking to see if the candidate will assert themselves. Will they take charge like a good salesperson and attempt to close the meeting and the deal?

So, similar to how a prospect may behave nearing the end of a meeting, I show a bit of discomfort, shift around in my chair, and try to make the candidate feel like we're running out of time. I am doing all of this looking to see (and truly hoping) the candidate will do what sales professionals do. Do they show initiative and take the lead? Are they gutsy and sophisticated enough to try to flesh out objections? Will they even attempt to try to close you on a next step, tell you why they are the best choice to hire, and ask for the business (the job)?

My sales fantasy in this situation is that a candidate would stop me right there, look me in the eye, assert control, and say, "Mike, I am very excited about this opportunity, and based on our conversation feel like I am the perfect fit for this position. Let me ask, do you have any concerns about my candidacy? Are there any weaknesses you perceive that I might be able to address for you?"

Be honest. Tell me you wouldn't fall out of your chair if a candidate said that to you. How amazingly wonderful would that be for a candidate, if before they tried to close you and ask for the job, they probed to uncover potential concerns (or objections) you might have. As I said, that would be a sales fantasy.

In my case, it's a little bit different when I am interviewing because I'm the third party—the consultant/coach, not the employer. I can't extend an offer to the candidate and don't have the authority to make the decision. I'm not the hiring manager. But, oh how I love it when a salesperson understands this and yet pushes on me anyway. One of the best things they could say at this point is, "Mike, I really enjoyed this conversation. Thanks for spending all this time talking sales with me. May I just ask: Will you be recommending me to the company/hiring manager?"

I love it when they push like this because it demonstrates that they understand the dynamic and that they are attempting to close me. They're looking to flesh out potential objections I may have and to gain a commitment. The strongest candidates will have the guts to ask if they're the best candidate and if I will be endorsing them to my client. And if at that point I don't say yes, they may even continue to push, attempting to do more discovery and uncover what concerns or objections I might have. That's great selling.

Let's close this chapter right back where it began. To win big as a sales manager, you must get the right people on your team. In the next chapter we will shift our attention to a little counterintuitive sales management secret that will drive both more results and more enjoyment of your job.

7

YOUR JOB WILL BE MORE FUN AND YOU WILL DRIVE MORE RESULTS SPENDING MORE TIME WITH YOUR BEST PEOPLE

SO FAR, I HAVE OFFERED UP A handful of contrarian and provocative perspectives to stir your thinking, but this chapter may contain the most counterintuitive sales management advice of all. To maximize job enjoyment and results, spend more time with your very best salespeople.

NOTHING HURTS MORE THAN LOSING A TOP PRODUCER

During workshops when discussing smart sales-talent management, I'll often ask managers which of these scenarios they dread more: losing a giant customer or losing an A player salesperson? The response from the group is almost unanimous.

They agree they would fare better losing a customer's business than losing one of their best sellers. I concur.

As difficult as it is for the person in charge of the team that drives revenue to choose losing business, even hypothetically, they agree it is generally easier to replace a customer than it is to replace a highly talented, top-producing salesperson! That is because the harsh reality is that there are no unemployed, A player salespeople. None. Zero. They don't exist. There is not a single top-performing seller out looking for a job. In fact, in the recent challenging labor environment, you would be hard pressed to find even a solid B player salesperson on the market.

Think, for a minute, about the consequences of that reality. If it is truly that challenging to replace solid sales talent, shouldn't there be implications for how managers invest their precious, limited time? Wouldn't it follow that as a group, managers must elevate their game when it comes to supporting and retaining their very best people? While the answer seems obvious, what confuses me is that most managers are not prioritizing time with top producers anywhere near the rate they should be.

SELFISH BENEFITS FROM SPENDING MORE TIME WITH YOUR BEST SELLERS

In the first chapter of *Sales Management. Simplified,* I document how I flailed around as a first-time sales leader. I tell the story of how after six months struggling mightily, I finally broke down, picked up the phone, and desperate for coaching called my dad.

My father, an experienced senior sales executive and master philosopher on all topics, listened intently as I poured out my frustration and confusion. Once I was done venting (basically begging for his insight and help), he let out an amused chuckle. I'm convinced to this day that he was pleased that his cocky son had been humbled a bit. He affirmed for me that I had now joined the ranks of the overwhelmed sales managers, and that conversation was a turning point. It began the long journey in my effort to master sales management. It also opened the door to more productive dialogue about sales management with my father.

In a subsequent check-in conversation as I was starting to get a bit of traction and a handle on my priorities, I asked my dad how I could become a more effective sales leader and when would I actually begin to enjoy my job? I was still carrying a ton of stress and working way more than I had as an individual contributor. He offered up a life-giving tidbit that stopped me dead in my tracks. If you had given me ten guesses as to what he would suggest, I would not have come up with it.

"That's simple," he said. "Spend more time with your best people."

I thought, this must be one of the worst pieces of advice I'd ever received. I didn't come right out and say it, but just sat there in silence, thinking, *Have you lost your mind? What is that going to accomplish? I'm barely treading water, stressed and struggling, and I'm desperate to become more, not less, effective, and you want me to go* play *with the people on the team who don't need my help? Gimme a break, Dad. So much for thinking you would continue to inspire or guide me.*

Picking up on my silence and nonresponse, my dad continued, "Mike, trust me on this. It's the opposite of how most managers behave. Everyone is overinvesting in their problem children, and half of that effort is wasted anyway. Stop spending so much energy on your people who are sucking the life out of you and reinvest it in your best people. Too many managers ignore their A players because they are doing fine and figure they don't need the help. So they let their star sellers fly around on autopilot without much direction. What I'm telling you is that *these are the people* who know what to do with your coaching. And when you really need more business, *these are the people* who know how to find it. You want to have more fun and more energy? You want to enjoy your job? If you want to drive more results, then spend more time with your best people."

That radical, counterintuitive advice served me incredibly well. The more time I spent with the best salespeople, the more fun I had, the more I learned about the business, and the more ideas I got for how to coach and train our average sellers. I also noticed that a good percentage of these top producers appreciated the attention, support, and challenge. Not all, but most did. And some made it their mission to *teach me right*—to show me what support they needed from the company to sell even more. They also took me into their best customers to show off how they grew the business, displaced competitors, took market share, and became trusted advisors to these accounts—all things that underperformers don't often accomplish. And because these top producers were not insecure, they also dragged me into their toughest accounts and even former accounts (lost customers), and into prospecting calls. Unlike underperforming reps, they were willing to show me where they were stuck, struggling, or trying to break in, and were more than happy for another brain and set of eyes to potentially help create a breakthrough.

Chalk another one up to my dad. He was right, and for the next fifteen years, I operated as a sales leader and later as a coach/trainer/consultant living out and preaching the sage advice he gave me: don't ignore your best people. They know what to do with your coaching. They know where to find the sales. And not only will they teach you how to lead better, but spending more time with them will dramatically increase your energy, fun, and job satisfaction.

I didn't have the empirical data to support my father's claim that managers who overinvest in their top salespeople drive more results, only plenty of anecdotal observations from my own experience as a leader and that of my clients in my consulting and coaching practice.

Fifteen years after my dad whispered the advice that helped alter the trajectory of my sales leadership career, I picked up a very large client in the world of big data. The company was seeking to create a sales destination culture (their term) and also help their managers master the best practices from my book, *Sales Management. Simplified.* The executives at this respected company took their own medicine and applied the same data analyses they offered clients to their own business. One of the areas they analyzed? Sales manager performance.

During a prep session with the senior leaders for the *Sales Management. Simplified* workshops I would be facilitating in several cities around the world, the head of sales for the Americas shared a fascinating report with me. The company studied where their two hundred global sales managers were spending their time and correlated the manager time analysis with sales team performance. The executive pulled up a summary that had this fascinating and affirming discovery highlighted and in bold:

> The company's highest-performing sales managers spent more than twice as much time with their highest-performing salespeople than managers of average and below-average performing teams spent with their top salespeople.

Finally! I finally had the data to back up my dad's theory and my own anecdotal observations. A world-class data analytics company verified what I intuitively knew to be true. The very best leaders (managers of the highest-performing teams) were spending more time with their very best people. Yes, counter-intuitive, but oh so valuable! I'm not sure I can shout this at you any louder, my new manager friend. Not only will you have more fun and enjoyment, but you will also drive more results when you spend more time with your very best salespeople.

NOT ONLY WILL YOU HAVE MORE FUN AND ENJOYMENT, BUT YOU WILL ALSO DRIVE MORE RESULTS WHEN YOU SPEND MORE TIME WITH YOUR VERY BEST SALESPEOPLE.

Before providing some practical tips for how to best support your best team members, allow me to offer a quick word of warning. As hard as I am trying to convince you to dedicate more time to retaining and maximizing the performance of your highest performers, please do not take this as a free pass to ignore underperformance. Managers absolutely must identify and address underperformance quickly, and as we will examine in the next chapter, allowing underperformance to go unaddressed is akin to sales management malpractice. It's not *or*. It's *and*. We should spend more time with our best people *and* we must also coach up or coach out those who are underperforming. That, along with getting the right people in the right roles, is how we become masters of smart sales-talent management and win big as managers.

HOW ARE YOU PERSONALLY SUPPORTING YOUR TOP-PRODUCING SALESPEOPLE?

Picture your very best salespeople. Say or write down the names of your A players. Do it. Name your best people—the ones you'd be devastated to lose.

And just for perspective, if you consider 20 percent or more to be A players, then consider yourself blessed. Most managers would rate less than 20 percent of their people as true A players.

Now that you have your best people listed on paper or pictured in your mind's eye, answer this all-important question: What are *you* doing to retain and maximize the performance of these A players?

The question is worded exactly as intended. Notice that it is not asking what the company is doing to keep and support your best people. Neither is it asking what the CEO (or owner) or the general manager is doing. Nor is it inquiring about initiatives that HR has put in place. Or about recognition programs and reward trips. Or compensation packages. Nope. The question is directed at one person—the most important person in this equation. You.

What are you personally doing to not only keep your best people happy, engaged, motivated, and on your team but also to maximize their results? As you reflect on what you are currently doing, or *should/could* be doing, my best coaching is that you must personalize your approach. I'm confident that your A players are diverse; they are not carbon copies of one another. Each has a unique bent, style, and desire. And they likely even differ in their motivations for success. You have different people who are wired differently, which requires that you treat them differently—as individuals.

Let me offer up myself as an example. There is a stereotype that *all* top salespeople love recognition. They live to be called up on stage and recognized for their outstanding contribution. *Nothing* is more important or motivating than winning the prize, trophy, or award and being named Salesperson of the Year in front of the entire organization. That may indeed be the case for some percentage of top-producing salespeople. I've seen it. I get it. And I've got nothing against spotlight-craving sales champions. But that's not me. In fact, while I was the top producer at a midsized direct marketing and fulfillment company, I came to abhor being recognized in front of my peers on the sales team or the entire company. As ultracompetitive as I am, the last thing I wanted was more attention. People were already envious enough of the numbers I was putting up, the attention I was getting, and the income they figured I was earning. There was no desire to give the haters even more reason to resent me.

Senior management understood the importance of treating different people differently, so executives made the effort to learn what made me and the other high performers tick. The chief operating officer must have studied me well because instead of praising his number one salesperson in public during all-hands meetings, he'd invite me to his office every four to six weeks. He correctly figured out that private words of appreciation and seeking my opinion and input were way more motivating to me than being publicly showered with praise. So the COO would sit me down, verbalize his appreciation for my contribution, show me the impact my sales were making on the overall company financial statement, and then wrap up these short get-togethers with two questions. First, he'd ask how he could help. Was there anything I needed from the company? And then typically, right as I was standing up to exit his office, he would ask my opinion on some big decision he was considering. Honestly, I don't know how much weight he gave my input, but he sure knew how to make me feel valued and important.

IT IS PERFECTLY ACCEPTABLE TO DISCRIMINATE BASED ON PERFORMANCE

The leaders at that company modeled an important principle, and it's the same principle I observe so many first-rate sales managers demonstrating too. They invest the time and mental energy getting to know all their people and, even more so, getting to know and understand their best people really well. "Relational Rent," as one of my mentors termed it, is paid with time. Money is not the currency of relationship. Time, care, and concern are.

The logical conclusion of what I am advocating is that you will invest more time with your top salespeople. You will get to know them better than others on your team, and because you know them better, you will adapt how you manage them. Dare I say, you will even give these top producers *special treatment.* You will serve and support them differently than you serve and support others. And I know as you are reading this that your *discrimination* antennae are going up. I can almost feel you getting uncomfortable. You may even be thinking, "Wait a minute, Mike. You are encouraging me to treat certain people on my team better than others, give them more support, or possibly even bend the rules for them."

You are correct. I'm absolutely saying that to you—as loudly as I can. And you are likely thinking that isn't right. That is not fair. That's discrimination. Discrimination is wrong. Are you trying to get me in trouble or fired?

Hear me clearly. While I am strongly advocating that you discriminate, I am certainly not suggesting you do it on the basis of gender, race, age, or religion. Not for a second. Far from it. But I am indeed begging you to discriminate based on one critical factor—performance! As far as I understand it, there is no law that prevents you from giving better treatment and more support to people on your team who deserve it because they've earned it. I repeat, they deserve special treatment because they have earned it.

BECOME THE BRIDGE TO THE DESIRED FUTURE FOR YOUR TOP PRODUCERS

Over the past decade I have been privileged to work with some of the strongest sales leaders on this planet. One of the best parts of doing what I do is the opportunity to observe and learn from the very best executives and managers—many of whom I'm convinced could out manage me any day of the week!

Mike Jeffrey is a vice president at Paychex and wise beyond his years. I'm not sure I've met a more articulate or purposeful sales leader. In every conversation he drops memorable gems, and I have lost count how often I quote him or refer to something brilliant he has shared while we were filming a roundtable discussion with my favorite, ridiculously talented sales leaders for a video series.

When Mike speaks, people not only listen, they take notes—a lot of notes. I certainly do. A few years back I specifically asked him about retaining top producers and what he was encouraging his sales managers to do to hang on to their best people. Paychex maintains a fabulous sales culture, and because the company has an excellent reputation as a training ground for young sales stars, other employers are always looking to poach their best sales reps.

Mike's response to my inquiry was prescient and powerful. Honestly, he raised the bar so high with what he's advocating managers do (become) to keep and grow their best people that it's helpful to view his advice as aspirational. His recommendation will stretch you and your thinking. It certainly challenged me.

Mike wants to see managers "become the bridge." We should strive to get to the place where we know our A players so well, and to earn such a position of trust, that they let us in on not only who they are and where they are, but where they want to go. Mike believes that when top salespeople share with us their professional and personal goals and see us not only as advocates but as facilitators who will help them achieve their desired future, then their success becomes our success. And when we become perceived as *the bridge* that helps take these uber talented salespeople from where they are today to where they want to be (their desired future state), they will not leave us. Not only won't they leave us, but they'll run through walls for us to produce maximum results because we have captured their hearts.

May I ask you to invest a few minutes pondering Mike Jeffrey's challenge? Yes, it's a high bar he set for us, so let's consider his challenge to *become the bridge* as aspirational. With that as the goal, what would it take to get to know your best people so well and for them to trust you to the extent that they begin to see you as that facilitator, as that bridge, who will take them from where they are today to where they want to be?

Let me address a concern that may be surfacing as you ponder building this type of relationship with a subordinate. I've had managers share their fear or discomfort toward building that level of bond with someone on their team. Some will ask if there is danger in becoming that close, even friends, with a top salesperson. This is a wise concern that demonstrates discernment and maturity.

While I am advocating a level of investment and support where you may become relationally closer to A players on your team, I am not encouraging you to focus on building a true (mutual) friendship per se. That is not the goal.

Is it possible that a genuine friendship emerges? Certainly. And there are potential pitfalls when that occurs. In full disclosure and transparency, however, looking back over my career, I certainly became friends with several of my best bosses and later with my best salespeople and have never once regretted it. Some have become lifelong friendships that have enriched my life. Just last year I was asked to give the eulogy at the funeral service for one of those A players from my very first sales management position. It had been twelve years since we worked together, but the bond we built and the friendship that resulted was genuine. Long after we both moved on from that company, the friendship remained—one that emerged as I sought to *become the bridge* for this very talented top performer. From my experience and perspective, the upside (both professional and personal) resulting from becoming the bridge for our best people far outweighs the complications a closer relationship might entail. Your best people have earned and deserve special treatment. The risk (and cost) of potentially losing them is far greater than the risk (and potential damage) from a friendship developing between you. If the payoff is retaining and maximizing the output of my very best salespeople, that is a bet and risk I am more than willing to take.

IF YOU'RE NOT SURE HOW TO SUPPORT YOUR A PLAYERS, JUST ASK THEM

Managers will occasionally tell me that they are unsure how to best support their best sellers. The desire is there but they are not confident about the right course of action to pursue. Some newer managers are also overly cautious about approaching top producers. They don't want to look foolish, and they are a bit intimidated. I understand. We don't want to be perceived as the naive newbie who is trying too hard but clueless about what our most valuable, often demanding and high-maintenance, people need.

Brace yourself for my earth-shattering advice. Ask them. Just ask them. I promise you that they will not only appreciate the inquiry, but they very likely already have a list, at least a mental list, ready to share with you.

You can do this by individually meeting one-by-one with your A players. But I suggest considering occasionally bringing all of your best people together. The very act of inviting your elite sellers to gather for an exclusive meeting demonstrates your intention to set them apart—and to lead them differently than others. Once together, make it exceedingly clear that you are there to listen. Share that you want to hear their thoughts and desires, that they've earned the right to be heard and supported. Inquire about what's in their way from having even bigger breakthroughs and significantly increasing their production. Ask what rules may need to change or what new tools would be beneficial. Encourage them to think and dream big, to get outside of the box. Make it abundantly clear to these winners that you have no intention of ignoring them just because they're doing well. You are committed to seeing them experience even higher levels of success and are willing to invest your time and effort making that happen.

> YOUR PRIMARY JOB AS THE SALES MANAGER IS TO INCREASE SALES. IT'S NOT TO CARETAKE A GROUP OF PEOPLE. IT'S NOT TO PLAY ADMINISTRATOR OR SUPERVISOR. YOUR JOB IS TO DRIVE MORE SALES.

This is a good time to remind you that your primary job as the sales manager is to increase sales. It's not to caretake a group of people. It's not to play administrator or supervisor. Your job is to drive more sales, and you accomplish that through the people on your team. There are no prizes for working longer hours than other managers or doing this the hard way. The best and strongest advice I can provide to help you drive more sales and have more fun while doing it is to Spend. More. Time. with your best people. This may seem contrarian and counterintuitive, but you will thank me later if you heed this advice. More fun and more results await you!

In the next chapter we will examine the extreme other end of the pendulum and the importance of quickly identifying and addressing underperformance.

8

IT IS SALES MANAGEMENT MALPRACTICE TO IGNORE UNDERPERFORMANCE

WHILE I TRULY HOPE YOU heed my encouragement in the previous chapter to increase your job satisfaction and your team's results by overinvesting in your top performers, there is a less enjoyable aspect of sales management that we now must tackle.

COMMON REASONS MANAGERS AVOID ADDRESSING UNDERPERFORMANCE

I have not surveyed the entire sales management population, but I can state this with a high degree of certainty: pretty much none of us likes having difficult conversations with the people on our team who are struggling and who are falling short of their goals.

There are many understandable reasons that we are uncomfortable confronting underperformance. Sometimes it's simply us. One reason we end up in a management role is because we are good with people: we like people, and people like us. It's not just that we were exceptional at our previous job or delivered great results; often it is because some senior leader in the organization appreciated our soft skills and viewed us as someone trustworthy of leading a team. A decent percentage of managers are wired like harmonizers and place a high value on maintaining relationships, so it should not be surprising that people with this makeup often struggle when it comes to pointing out someone's failings. We enjoy the coaching, cheerleading, and the celebrating but not the conflict from confronting someone with their unimpressive results. That is precisely why many of us protect ourselves from feeling like the bad guy and shy away from putting underperformers on the spot.

Other managers avoid difficult conversations because they are not sure how to approach them. Good accountability and confronting underperformance have not been modeled well by their own managers in the past. Therefore, they hesitate to initiate this type of conversation with people on their team because they have no framework for how it should look.

Managers are also well aware that salespeople, particularly underperforming salespeople, typically excel at baffling them with bullshit. Struggling sellers somehow find ways to become masters at making excuses. It's a special skill that almost every underperforming salesperson acquires. They may not be succeeding at closing sales, but they sure are adept at selling their managers on why they missed their numbers! Assuming the meeting will be pointless and rightfully concerned that underperformers will push back, whine, complain, point fingers, and blame everything and everyone but themselves, managers decide to avoid confronting underperformance head-on and instead intentionally look the other way.

I've had managers ask me point blank why they should even bother addressing underperformance when they don't believe anything will change. Rather than viewing themselves as leaders and agents of change and believing that both their coaching and accountability sessions could affect a struggling salesperson's performance, they prefer to simply accept the fact that this person will fail. I'm not even sure how to respond to managers with such fatalistic, defeatist attitudes. Why would you even accept a leadership role if you do not believe you can improve the performance of the people entrusted to you?

Beyond the reasons described previously, by far the most dangerous, dare I say deadly, reason that managers tell me they are hesitant to properly address underperformance is fear—fear that the underperformer will not only balk at being confronted with their failure but that the underperformer will potentially begin looking for another job. Before I even begin unpacking the line of pathetic reasoning managers offer up as justification for permitting underperformance to continue unaddressed, please pause for a moment and play out this line of thinking to its logical conclusion. The leader of the team, whose primary job is to drive increased results, hesitates to discuss performance with someone who is failing. And just in case you think that the word *failing* is too harsh or that I used it casually here, let me be exceedingly clear. *Failing* is the correct, appropriate word. Failing to hit the goal, or achieve quota, is failing. Therefore, fear that a failing salesperson may not appreciate being confronted with the facts/data/truth and might begin to look for employment elsewhere is not acceptable justification for ignoring the underperformance! Furthermore, the manager's oversensitivity that the failing salesperson will resist or rebuff additional coaching and accountability is simply foolish. It's a silly, false, circular argument that gets us nowhere. If you cannot address underperformance because you are afraid your weakest team member might be offended or leave, then your fatalistic approach dooms you to failure as a leader.

Some managers are undeterred when I challenge their ludicrous assertion that they are basically powerless to effect change, and they double down attempting to persuade me how costly it is to lose a salesperson, even one who is failing. I have heard some version of this more than you want to know: "Mike, you don't understand. I can't afford to lose a salesperson right now. If I were to sit down with Johnny (the name I use in my writing and workshops for the underperformer) and show him where he stands compared to others on the team and make it clear that he needs to raise his game and production—even though I'm willing to help with extra coaching and accountability—I am deathly afraid that I will lose him. He may not say it right away, but he'll immediately start looking to leave."

At this point, I typically raise my eyebrows in confusion, peer out over my reading glasses and reply with one word stated as a question "*And . . .* ?"

The manager continues whining about the pending doomsday scenario. "I'm already overloaded and if I get the feeling that Johnny is going to bail on me, then I have to ramp up the recruiting engine. I don't have time for that. Plus, when Johnny does resign, I will get the third degree from HR, and it will also ding my turnover percentage. And then my life will really be hell because I'm the one who will end up covering the empty position, and my phone will blow up with service needs from Johnny's customers. Interviewing will be a huge headache, and then once I finally settle on a candidate, I will have to deal with the hassle of onboarding, orienting, and getting the new hire up to speed." At this point, I shake my head and increase my intensity. "You realize that what you just described is complete and utter sales management malpractice. It is also an abdication of your role. You've adopted a defeatist attitude. You talk like you have zero ability to influence Johnny's future performance and that you have no desire to coach him up to an acceptable level. And worst of all, you have decided that it's too much hassle to do what professional managers do, and because you don't want to deal with recruiting, hiring, and onboarding, you are going to pretend that this will somehow magically fix itself. All the while, you are destroying whatever winning culture may exist on your team and, without actually saying the words, communicating to everyone on the team that failure is acceptable."

UNADDRESSED UNDERPERFORMANCE DAMAGES CULTURE AND MORALE

The damage to team culture when leaders let underperformance go unaddressed cannot be overstated. Let me use a sports analogy to illustrate. Imagine that you are the manager for an elite soccer (football to the rest of the world outside the US) club that plays in a select (highly competitive) league. Again, this is not the *church league;* picture this as Premier League. There are no *participation trophies,* and everyone pays close attention to the score at every match and to the league standings. The goal is to win the championship. When you were selected to lead the team, ownership explained in no uncertain terms that the goal is to win.

Now imagine that you have a player on the pitch whom we'll call Johnny. He's your weakest player, and you typically play Johnny at left back. The problem is that just about every time Johnny gets the ball, he loses possession to the other team. Johnny is a liability on the pitch, and everyone on your team sees it and knows it. Yet, regardless of the circumstance, score, time remaining on the clock, or the importance of this particular game, there's Johnny (poorly) occupying the left back position.

My sales manager friend, what are the consequences of this soccer manager's mismanagement of his team? What message is the manager sending to his other players by leaving Johnny in the lineup? How much extra pressure does each of the players adjacent to Johnny carry because of his inability to possess the ball? How much harder do others need to work to make up for Johnny's mistakes? When the team loses a match because of Johnny's repeated underperformance, what do you think happens to morale? And when the season ends and two of the best players announce that they are leaving to play for another club because winning is one of their core values, what affect will that have on other players' attitudes and excitement?

Don't be tempted to dismiss the point here because you're a sales manager not a soccer club manager. This isn't a cute sports story. This is exactly what takes place on sales teams when management avoids addressing underperformance. Even if you're not speaking the words, everyone *hears* the message clearly: failure is acceptable. And if management has to lean harder on high performers to deliver even more results because others are not pulling their weight, so be it. And if we lose an A player or two because they want to play alongside other winners on a winning team, so be it. And if we don't earn the discretionary portion of our bonus because the bottom performers on our team dragged down overall results, so be it.

I am not sure there is a more powerful force than the culture of a sales team. When it's a strong, healthy, energized, winning, celebrating, and self-policing culture, it's a sight to behold and an unstoppable force. But all of that can be destroyed by management turning a blind eye to underperformance.

Let me add an additional caution and insight regarding underperformance and highly variable compensation plans. When all, or the vast majority, of a salesperson's compensation is variable, there can be a temptation to ignore when someone is not delivering the desired results. Managers are tempted to say that it doesn't matter if salespeople fail here because they only get paid if they succeed. That may indeed be true—at least the part about not paying people who are not earning commission. But commission is not the only cost. What about the desk (the spot in your lineup) they're taking up? What about the oxygen they're breathing (and polluting)? What about the internal resources being wasted instead of redirected to others who are producing? And most importantly, what about the message to the team that it's okay to fail here?

Argument presented. The prosecution rests. The evidence is overwhelming. Case closed. Ignoring underperformance is indeed management malpractice.

WHY DO WE TOLERATE UNDERPERFORMANCE IN SALES BUT NOT OTHER AREAS?

As you've figured out by now, I am often confused. One of the things that most confuses me is that in businesses with very high standards for excellence and performance, somehow salespeople get a pass. Struggling sellers often go months, quarters, or even years without being confronted by their managers. Perhaps there is so much mystery (confusion) about what drives success in sales, there is an overriding hesitancy to quickly call out underperformance and work to turn it around.

What a contrast to other departments or positions. Imagine a software engineer on a team developing code. At month-end, management does a quality control review and identifies that one particular developer wrote the most bugs into the code. How long do you think it would take before the team leader sat that developer down to address the poor quality of his work?

Similarly, if a midlevel accountant were producing inaccurate month-end financial statements, and this accountant's mistakes were being caught either by the bank reviewing the financials or by the CFO, how long before this accountant would be confronted by their manager? And how quickly would some type of coaching ensue to ensure that this did not happen again? Or what if there were a shipping clerk in the warehouse who continued to mispack boxes? Or a technician in the service department who regularly returned machines to customers without having properly diagnosed and fixed the problem?

Exactly. The correct answer in all of these scenarios is a nanosecond. Whether it's the software engineer, the accountant, the shipping clerk, or the technician, no one would think it is reasonable to allow these people to continue underperforming in their jobs. Their failures would immediately be confronted, and each person's leader would spearhead the effort to coach them up to acceptable levels of performance. Shouldn't we, as sales managers, be similarly quick to identify and address underperformance? It is hard to argue otherwise.

REGULAR RESULTS-FOCUSED ACCOUNTABILITY MEETINGS SET THE STAGE FOR CONFRONTING UNDERPERFORMERS

Furthermore, if managers are regularly conducting the simple one-on-one accountability meetings as outlined in chapter 3, it is only natural to address repeated underperformance. Play out this scenario with me. You sit with Johnny for your regular, formal, scheduled accountability meeting. You start by reviewing his actual results. Results against goals and compared to others on the team. Johnny missed his numbers and is trailing behind others on the team. It's now out in the open, and together you discuss what happened. Fast-forward to next month's accountability meeting. You sit with Johnny again. He misses the goal again. You discuss the underperformance—and then continue through the progression reviewing his pipeline and activity. You make it clear that he needs to pick up the pace and look forward to seeing him improve and achieve his target next month. And yet once more, in month three you sit with Johnny for your regular, formal accountability session, and he, as usual, fell short of what was expected. Different month. Same story. It's the third consecutive month Johnny has failed.

My question for you, my first-time manager friend, is simple and pointed. How long are you going to suffer the fool gladly? Seriously. How many more months are you going to allow this to repeat itself before you change the dialogue with Johnny?

Let me ask you again. For how long are you (the leader) going to allow Johnny to fail before you (the leader) do something about it? How long must his underperformance persist before you change your approach with him? To me, it sure seems like after a few months of these *Groundhog Day* accountability meetings, we are getting mighty close to living out *the definition of insanity* that makes us all chuckle—doing the same thing over and over yet expecting a different result. Something needs to change.

CHANGING THE CONVERSATION TO BEGIN COACHING UP UNDERPERFORMERS

Since we (leaders) are of sound mind, the responsibility is ours to change the conversation from simply reviewing results, pipeline/progress, and activity to one where we make it exceedingly clear to our struggling salesperson that performance must improve.

Before outlining what this very clear communication should look and sound like, let me offer a few reminders about approach and tone when it comes to holding people accountable for delivering results. For most managers, this is one of the most difficult parts of the job and something that feels foreign because as individual contributors we were not tasked with confronting colleagues about their underperformance.

Similar to my suggested tone that we should employ when conducting the regular accountability meeting, this initial "coaching-up conversation" should also be nonemotional. We've already established that many managers, particularly those who are more relational, don't look forward to difficult conversations, which is part of the reason that they avoid initiating the dialogue. They do not like confronting people. But not wanting to confront someone is not a "Get Out of Jail Free" card. As leaders, we don't get to punt because, as we have already established, that is sales management malpractice. It's our responsibility to address the situation and the salesperson head-on. Again, our job as sales managers is to deliver results—to win through our people. When someone is losing, we must address it. But that does not mean that we have to freak out on someone. There is no need to demonstrate anger or even disappointment toward the struggling salesperson. Please hear me. Confrontation does not necessarily mean conflict. I am not advocating aggression, blaming, or shaming. To the contrary, I am encouraging you to offer help to someone who needs it.

Addressing underperformance head-on and offering to help turn it around can be a quite positive experience. Shortly, I will share a memorable success story I heard from a previous underperformer who matured into a sales rockstar and successful senior executive after getting tough love and serious coaching up from a manager!

Let me also remind you that just because the time has come to change your approach does not mean you are on the path to firing this struggling person. The true goal of confronting unacceptable performance is to turn around the person who is failing. We should not view addressing underperformance as the initial step in the process for terminating someone's employment. It may turn out to be the case, but that is most definitely not the goal of beginning the coach-up process. The primary purpose for confronting underperformance, instead of allowing it to go unaddressed, is exactly what I call it: "coaching up" the struggling salesperson to an acceptable level of performance. That's the whole point!

THE TRUE GOAL OF CONFRONTING UNACCEPTABLE PERFORMANCE IS TO TURN AROUND THE PERSON WHO IS FAILING. WE SHOULD NOT VIEW ADDRESSING UNDERPERFORMANCE AS THE INITIAL STEP IN THE PROCESS FOR TERMINATING SOMEONE'S EMPLOYMENT.

My hope is that reminding you of the proper motivation for confronting underperformance serves as an incentive to do so quickly instead of avoiding it. Again, I am not instructing you to terminate someone in a sales slump. If you are a low-conflict, more relational person, there is not a need to tie yourself into knots and suffer a week of sleepless nights before sitting down with Johnny to change the dialogue. You are not firing Johnny; you are looking to help alter his trajectory by directly addressing the facts, the numbers, and outlining a plan to get him on the right path. And your motivation for initiating the conversation is pure. It's for Johnny's sake, the good of your team, and the culture. Oh yes, it's also your job.

And honestly, you owe it to Johnny. I mean it. You owe him the professional courtesy of confronting him with his underperformance. You owe him the opportunity to right the ship. And I truly believe that you owe him your very best help to make it happen.

You may have inherited Johnny when you assumed leadership of the team, and if that's the case then it is highly possible that Johnny was not coached well in the past. Maybe your predecessor did not invest the time to develop Johnny's skills or, even more likely, looked the other way when he continued to underdeliver. Or maybe it was you who hired Johnny, but if you're being completely transparent, you have not (to this point) devoted the necessary time and coaching to help him succeed. Regardless of what has led to this crossroad, the point is that you are now here, and it's on you to do what responsible leaders do.

Starting the coach-up conversation is often the hardest part for managers. My advice is not to beat around the bush. Get right into the facts in a no-nonsense manner. Don't turn this conversation into something more dramatic than it needs to be. It doesn't require a long setup, and the less emotional, the better. Remember, Johnny knows he is underperforming. He also knows that you know he is underperforming because you have been pointing this out to him on a regular basis. There is no *breaking news* here, and the fact that you are sitting Johnny down for this dialogue should be a surprise to nobody.

Bring the data (reports) to the meeting and start by simply stating the facts. If Johnny has missed his numbers for four consecutive months, then show him the numbers. Point out where he stands compared to others on the team. And if his pipeline (progress), as a leading indicator of future performance, is not sufficient and is predicting that he will continue to fall short of his goals, show him that as well. Don't embellish or exaggerate the data. Just present it. Clearly communicate to Johnny that the current trajectory cannot continue and that *we* need to get this turned around as quickly as possible. And it is absolutely okay to say "we" because you, the manager, are a significant contributor to this coach-up process you're initiating.

Once you have presented the facts to Johnny and made it abundantly clear that his current level of performance is not acceptable, paint the picture of what acceptable performance looks like and let him know you are committed to helping him get there. This is critical because if this coaching up is going to succeed, the underperformer needs to grasp that there is additional help on the way.

At this early stage in the conversation, it is common for the manager to read into Johnny's reaction, attempting to get a feel for whether he understands the gravity of the situation and accepts the premise that his underperformance will no longer be tolerated. My coaching is to resist your instincts at this point. Hold off trying to discern if Johnny is tracking with you—yet. For a few more minutes, give him the benefit of the doubt even if his body language is screaming that he's not on board with whatever you are about to present. Let's give him the opportunity to comprehend the entire picture, including both what you are committing to and what you are asking him to commit to, before judging his reaction.

OFFER TO DOUBLE YOUR COACHING AND ACCOUNTABILITY IN RETURN FOR THE STRUGGLING SALESPERSON'S COMMITMENT

Congratulations. You have already made it past the hardest part—the point that most managers never reach. Instead of turning a blind eye to repeated underperformance, you have addressed it head-on. From here forward, the process practically takes care of itself.

After reviewing the data and confronting Johnny with the facts, it is now time to calmly pivot the conversation to what comes next:

1. Offer to double up on the amount of coaching you provide Johnny (this is the literal *coaching up*) over the defined coach-up period.
2. Make it clear that during this period you will also double up on your accountability sessions with Johnny.
3. Secure a commitment from Johnny for both increased activity and increased achievement during this defined period of time.

It's that simple. Rather than ignoring Johnny's struggles, you will be directly engaging with him. His underperformance has been exposed and labeled as exactly what it is. Now it's out in the light. No pretending. No shame. No condemnation. Again, the primary purpose for beginning the coach-up process is to turn Johnny's performance around, even if it's just temporarily.

Restate that you are going to provide extra coaching and guidance because you want to see Johnny succeed. Set the expectation that you will be spending more time with him and that this additional coaching may take various forms. More precall planning. More working alongside Johnny to observe and assist. More debriefing. More strategizing opportunities. Maybe even more training (or retraining). It's imperative that Johnny understands that you are in this with him and that your desire is to see him succeed.

Along with the additional coaching comes increased visibility and more frequent accountability. The reality is that

Johnny's struggles have *earned* him more attention on his performance. Therefore, it's completely understandable that concurrent with the extra help you are providing, you will be diving in deeper and more regularly to monitor his progress. Again, this is not inappropriate micromanagement. It's Johnny's own lack of results that have earned him this extra oversight. So let him know you will be more closely tracking with his progress and meeting with him more often.

The third critical component of this coach-up process is securing Johnny's commitment to more effort, more progress, and more results. There must be mutuality if this process is going to work. You, the leader, offered your commitment first, and now it is time to secure Johnny's commitment to the process. There is no point in doubling up on your effort and workload attempting to save Johnny if he isn't interested in the life preserver you are tossing him.

It's important that you spell out your expectations for Johnny's improved performance. Show him what acceptable achievement looks like—and not just *effort* and activity but actual sales progress and actual results. Restate your commitment to extra coaching and accountability, and make it clear that you are asking him to commit to hitting those targets.

THE UNDERPERFORMER MUST BUY IN TO THE COACH-UP PLAN

Earlier I suggested to not judge Johnny's initial reaction to being confronted with his underperformance. That's because I have witnessed the struggling salesperson's emotional response change once the gravity of the situation and the manager's reasonable offer sinks in. After an initial strong, defensive reaction, cooler heads often prevail as the seller processes the dialogue and sees that not only are they not being terminated but also that this is not just some boilerplate HR-driven *performance improvement plan*—the kind everyone perceives as a formality that companies deploy to protect themselves. No, this is something very different. This is not a legal/compliance cover-your-ass-so-you-don't-get-sued plan; it is a human manager offering significant assistance to a human salesperson who needs it.

THIS IS NOT A LEGAL/COMPLIANCE COVER-YOUR-ASS-SO-YOU-DON'T-GET-SUED PLAN; IT IS A HUMAN MANAGER OFFERING SIGNIFICANT ASSISTANCE TO A HUMAN SALESPERSON WHO NEEDS IT.

And this is exactly why we must get the underperformer's complete buy-in to what we are offering. So we conclude this direct conversation by asking Johnny for two things. First, we ask him straight-up if he's committed to improving his performance. "Johnny, I need to know if you are on board with what I have outlined for you today. I am committed to making the investment to help get your performance where it needs to be. I will absolutely be doubling up on coaching and accountability with you because I want to see you succeed. But for this to work, it requires mutuality. I need to hear from you. Are you 100 percent committed to putting in the extra effort to turn this around, and are you agreeable to the additional coaching and accountability from me?"

The second thing we will request from Johnny is a written plan. Notice that I am not asking you to write a plan for Johnny's success. Oh no. We've already expressed what we are contributing to this coach-up process. To ensure Johnny has indeed bought in and is worthy of our extra time and focus, we must secure both his verbal affirmation and a written commitment. So ask him to draft a brief plan outlining how he is going to get his results where they need to be, and have him include specifics about activity levels and other appropriate metrics (pipeline health, opportunity creation, deals reaching certain stages, and so on).

How Johnny responds to your two requests is critical. This coach-up process is a two-way street. There has to be mutuality or there is no reason to do it. It's imperative to secure Johnny's verbal and written commitment to the plan. If he's on board, then it is all systems go. But if you are not pleased with how Johnny responds, it's a totally different story. If Johnny starts spewing excuses or attacking the company or declaring how this isn't fair or explaining how you don't understand the situation, that is more than just a yellow light. That is a gigantic red flag. Full stop.

Similarly, if Johnny manages to fake his way through the verbal agreement but comes back with a garbage written plan that demonstrates neither serious effort nor commitment to the process, doesn't that tell us everything we need to know? When someone who's failing his way out of the job gets tossed a lifeline and doesn't have the respect or sense to grab hold of it and demonstrate his commitment (let alone his appreciation) for the opportunity to save himself, that is a pretty strong indicator that nothing is going to change.

So pay close attention to how Johnny responds to your request for mutuality. If he buys in, that's fantastic and exactly what we hoped. You then should be more than willing to jump in with both feet for a defined period to offer massive assistance. By all means, begin immediately. But if Johnny's reaction communicates that he isn't all that interested in your investment or committing to his extra effort, then there is zero reason (or incentive) to begin coaching him up. In that case, I strongly recommend that you do whatever your company requires in order to terminate Johnny. Do not expend one ounce of energy or one additional minute attempting to get him going in the right direction. You have given him an amazing opportunity, and he has thumbed his nose at it and at you. His performance is unacceptable. You have made it clear that it is unacceptable. You have offered to help him, and he, by his response, has rejected your offer. It's now time to move Johnny out.

THE END RESULT IS ALWAYS GOOD

I offer you one last bit of strong encouragement. If you are not quite sure whether it's time to address an underperformer's underperformance, then it's time.

There are two possible outcomes from putting someone on a coach-up plan. The first (and most desirable) outcome is that the plan works! The manager's extra investment into coaching and accountability combined with the commitment from the struggling salesperson pays off. At the conclusion of the coach-up period, the salesperson is now performing at an acceptable level—at least temporarily. It's a complete win-win. You've raised the salesperson's game, saved them their job, and potentially altered the trajectory of their career. And as you'll see in the example that follows, that's not an overstatement.

The other possible outcome is that the coach-up plan fails. Even with all the extra effort from both the coach and coachee, the salesperson was not able to increase performance to an acceptable level. While this is not the desired outcome, it's still a good outcome because we have clarity; we have a definitive answer. This salesperson is not going to succeed in the job, and it's time to set this person free to succeed elsewhere. While this was not the outcome we were hoping for, we can sleep well because as the leader we have done our job. We not only addressed underperformance (protecting our culture and sending a critical message to the team), we also made the supreme effort to save our struggling seller. We have done all we could and now know that we must replace our Johnny.

Nothing good comes from avoiding (or delaying) the conversation and the coach-up process. If you are not certain whether to initiate coaching a person up, then do it because the end result is always good.

Let me conclude this challenging chapter with a coach-up success story to encourage you. I am always amused, and even a bit amazed, when I lead discussions with sales managers about addressing underperformance. Along with all of the frustrating examples of avoiding underperformers, I also get to hear about some pretty amazing successes. And while it's fun to hear managers talk (brag) about how they've turned around struggling salespeople, the most powerful stories I have heard recently were from people who were on the other end of the coach-up conversation! It's one thing to hear from a manager about saving Johnny and turning around his career, but it's exponentially more powerful to hear the story from Johnny himself—particularly when Johnny has become a sales rockstar or is now a senior vice president at a billion-dollar organization.

I was leading a full-day workshop for sixty managers at a company in Texas. We had just finished outlining much of what's in this chapter and were doing an exercise about which reports (data) are most important to bring to the initial coach-up conversation. We were also practicing how to begin the dialogue with a struggling salesperson. Just as one of the managers inquired about how direct we should be when confronting the underperformer, the senior vice president stood up and walked toward me at the front of the room. As the facilitator, I love when this happens because it tells me that we're on target and that what I'm teaching has struck a chord with senior leadership.

It was obvious that I needed to step aside and let the SVP take the floor. Looking out at his sales management team, he began, "I am going to tell you a quick story to reinforce this concept that Mike is working so hard for you to grasp. The only other person in this room who knows this story is our CEO. Sales managers, I was Johnny. Thirty years ago, I was the struggling, young, somewhat apathetic sales rep. I was maybe six months into the job, and my manager called me in to his office. He told me that he liked me and that he thought that I had promise and potential, but neither my effort nor results were cutting it. He told me he was disappointed that I was cutting corners and that I hadn't learned more about our product or improved at conducting sales calls. He told me to study harder, to learn the business, and to practice my craft. He wanted to see that I was serious about sales. He then said that we would be meeting one-on-one every week to review my progress and so that he could answer my questions. My manager finished the conversation by saying that he thought I had what it took to be really good, that he expected a lot more from me, and that he'd see me next week."

The SVP paused and then pointed at my slide on the screen that simply said: Ignoring Underperformance = Sales Management Malpractice. He concluded by saying, "I give that first manager of mine all the credit in the world for not allowing me to slack. And because he didn't ignore my underperformance, I'm standing before you today. I never, ever, ever, would be in this job today if not for that man."

From Johnny the Underperformer to Senior Vice President. If that story isn't incentive to address underperformance, nothing will be.

9

USE THE MASSIVE EMOTIONAL AND MENTAL BANDWIDTH YOU OCCUPY IN YOUR SALESPEOPLE'S HEARTS AND MINDS WISELY

CHAPTER 8 WAS HARD CORE. We tackled a critical sales management function and stressed the importance of remaining unemotional, particularly when confronting underperformance. And while that is a proven sales management best practice, in this chapter I offer you a stark contrast, swinging the pendulum in the opposite direction.

YOU ARE LEADING HUMAN BEINGS, NOT ROBOTS

Experience confirms that managers must conduct accountability meetings and confront underperformance solely based on the facts. However, I am compelled to suggest that this may be *the only time* managers should ignore a seller's emotional state. Salespeople are not unemotional beings. They are not robots. They are human beings and often the type of humans who are the most emotional! Wouldn't you agree that many people end up in sales because of their passion and emotional intelligence? In just about every sales role I observe, even in highly technical environments, EQ trumps IQ as a determinant of sales success. Emotions, and the emotional state of a salesperson, matter deeply.

In fact, I ask you to contrast the stereotypical personality characteristics of engineers, accountants, and project managers with those of salespeople. Point made? As I've written before, it is relatively common to find miserable accountants who, while emotionally detached from their jobs, still perform excellent accounting work, but I've yet to identify a single highly successful miserable salesperson. Selling requires emotional involvement.

Many years ago, I worked for an amazing sales leader. Donnie Williams, who was a great vice president of sales, friend, mentor, and later a business partner during my first stint as a coach and consultant, understood the emotional makeup of the salesperson better than anyone. Donnie would often preach these two powerful reminders using various parts of our anatomy to communicate his message:

1. Sales, particularly sales success, is often more about the heart than the head.
2. Sales management is the fine art of balancing encouraging the heart and kicking the ass.

Part of the reason Donnie was so successful as both an internal sales leader and as a consultant is because he understood and masterfully applied these truths whether leading his own sales teams or helping other executives and managers lead theirs. In a moment, I'll circle back to specifically address the balance Donnie advocates in point 2. But first allow me to unpack the thesis for this chapter:

> Frontline sales managers occupy way more space (mental and emotional bandwidth) in their people's minds and hearts than they're typically aware of or than they appreciate.

If you doubt this, even a bit, take a few minutes to reflect on how often your own current boss comes to mind—or how frequently a previous boss might pop into your thoughts. And it's not just the mental real estate that leaders occupy. What about your emotional reaction to your boss's comments, notes, praises, critiques, assistance, or lack thereof? Remember how badly you want to please them or how frustrated you get when not receiving praise and recognition you feel that you deserve? Or on the flip side, how far did their recognition or encouragement go? How deeply appreciative were you after receiving positive affirmation for a job well done? How much more motivated to work hard and drive results were you when you *felt* known, valued, and appreciated by your direct leader? So if these questions run through your mind regarding your own boss or leader, you better believe that those whom you lead have the same questions and concerns swirling in their mind. All. The. Time.

Sales manager friend, this is a weighty responsibility. Whether you are yet keenly aware of it or not, as the team leader, you take up significant mental and emotional bandwidth in your people's minds and hearts, and that is why it is imperative we heed Donnie Williams's advice to balance our approach.

THERE IS NOTHING MUTUALLY EXCLUSIVE ABOUT MAINTAINING A HIGH-PERFORMANCE, KICK-ASS SALES CULTURE AND CARING DEEPLY FOR THE PEOPLE ON YOUR TEAM

A bright, bold, young, new female sales leader asked the simplest, yet most profound, question during a recent sales leadership event I was hosting. "Mike, I am completely bought-in on the topic of accountability, but how do you balance accountability and empathy? How do I demonstrate that I care about the person while holding their feet to the fire for achieving results and hitting the number?"

Best. Question. Ever. Truly, this is *the question* every sales leader should be asking. And that is exactly what Donnie preaches with his simple, pithy declaration that our job as sales managers is to deftly balance kicking the ass and encouraging the heart.

My slightly less simple spin is something that I preach to every executive and manager who has ears to hear: there is nothing, and I mean nothing, mutually exclusive about being intensely focused on goals and results and posting reports and scorecards everywhere while fostering a pro-sales and pro-salesperson, caring community! You can (and must) conduct effective and efficient one-on-one accountability meetings laser focused on an individual seller's results and pipeline health and, when necessary, activity. That's nonnegotiable, and as strongly stated in chapter 3, *your most important job* is ensuring that your people are doing their job.

But at the same time, you can (and must) create a supportive, caring, and dare I say, even loving environment where salespeople are valued and respected!

There isn't a more powerful force than a sales culture that gets this balance right. Fun. Energetic. High standards. Keeps score. Celebrates success. Supportive. Self-polices. Proud. Practices hard. Pushes one another. Sense of community. Caring. This is exactly the type of environment where great people desire to work because they not only want to win but also desperately want to feel like they're part of something that is bigger than themselves.

The healthiest sales cultures have both pieces: kick ass and results focused, while also enjoying the sense of camaraderie as a team and maintaining a pro-salesperson, supportive environment! In fact, the single strongest sales culture I've encountered balanced this better than any organization I've observed in my thirty-year career. After just two days on-site, I told their CEO that if I knew how much fun it would be working with his team and how much I was going to learn, I wouldn't have charged them for the engagement.

I wasn't kidding. The experience was that mind blowing. From the moment I set foot in the building it felt like I should take my shoes off because I was standing on holy sales ground. The culture was that good. That loud. Scoreboards on every wall. One-on-one accountability meetings executed to perfection. Planning meetings between the CEO and top producers that made my jaw drop as he simultaneously stretched, challenged, coached, supported, encouraged, and edified his people. Sales team meetings where *everyone* participated and that beautifully balanced positivity and practice with pointed feedback. I had never seen salespeople and success honored and celebrated in such a big way. This culture was truly the perfect picture of all that is good in sales. I go into this story in more detail in chapter 18 of *Sales Management. Simplified*, but will recap here as the best example I have seen of achieving this delicate balance in practice.

The leaders in this organization had great awareness and respect for how much head and heart space they occupied in their people, and they were absolutely committed to continually investing in the emotional connection between seller and sales leader. They neither took for granted nor abused the influence they wielded, and everyone benefited. I had never witnessed such an engaged and invested sales team. These leaders took Mike Jeffrey's exhortation from chapter 7 to "become the bridge" for their people to an entirely different level, and I am convinced that is the predominant reason members of this sales team produced results at triple the rate of the average salesperson in their industry. Leadership matters, and when leaders deftly use the space they occupy in their people's minds and hearts for good, great things happen.

THE TRANSFORMATIVE POWER OF YOUR PEOPLE KNOWING THAT YOU ARE "FOR THEM"

I have both personally and professionally benefited from having mentors and managers who made a tremendous impact in my life—from summer camp counselors to sales team leaders, chief executive officers to church pastors who not only invested in my development but also made it crystal clear that they were "for me."

It is hard to find the words sufficient to properly articulate the transformative power of having leaders in your life who want the best for you, sometimes even more than you want it for yourself. And while I could fill an entire book (and someday maybe will) with the life-changing lessons gleaned (and outcomes achieved) from those leaders who poured themselves into me and made a significant dent in my life, there is one particular example that beautifully illustrates the point I so badly want sales managers to grasp.

In late 2004 my family started attending a relatively new church in the area. We were drawn to it for many reasons, and my wife and I jumped in with both feet to serve in any way we could. The church was not only young in its existence, but its leaders and members were relatively young too. Those first few years at the church were an amazing season of growth for us as a family, and because we were a bit older than the average member (and even the leaders) and very much aligned with the mission, values, and culture of the church, Katie and I were entrusted with various opportunities to lead.

Of all the life-giving aspects of our involvement in that growing church, my most meaningful personal relationship developed with a man named Steve Miller. Steve was the executive pastor, which basically meant he was the glue of the organization. While the visionary lead pastor was doing his thing preaching, teaching, casting vision, and so on, two critical responsibilities fell to Steve. He was the guardian of the culture as the church grew quickly, and he *led the leaders* of the various ministries. In other words, without Steve there would have been chaos, very little of what needed to get done would have been executed, and the organization would have spun out of control and lost its way.

My early relationship with Steve can best be described as mutual mentorship. He's ten years younger than I am, so as we spent more time together and grew close, it was only natural that I would offer wisdom and perspective on topics ranging from parenting to financial planning. And as he got to know me better, he began pushing me into positions of more significant leadership in the church and mentoring me every step of the way. That is when I truly began to benefit from his brilliance as a leader. In fact, I'm not sure if at any time in my life I've been led as well as Steve led me.

One of the things that Steve not only taught but also modeled was this reality: *leadership is a series of hard conversations.* And whether he was sending me into a difficult conversation or, as was more often the case, initiating one with me (to coach, challenge, or even correct me), Steve Miller walked the talk. But more than any leader with whom I've closely worked (including CEOs of billion-dollar corporations) he had the uncanny ability to help you see why you were being challenged (stretched), and why it was in both your best interest and that of the organization.

To say that Steve pushed me past my comfort zone would be an understatement. From sending me into hospitals to pray with critically ill members, to leading important ministries, to entrusting and coaching me through opening and leading a new campus location (all of which I felt woefully ill equipped and unprepared to handle), he managed to get me to do it (successfully) with a willing heart.

What was Steve Miller's secret? How did he get me, and many others, to go above and beyond? How did he somehow manage to make me feel good after taking sandpaper to my rough edges in a coaching conversation or challenging me when I didn't give something or someone the attention they deserved? The answer is simple. In just about every conversation Steve communicated in no uncertain terms that He. Was. For. Me. For all the years I have known and loved this man, the one expression that pops to mind any time I think of Steve is this, "Mike, I am for you."

Getting emotional as I recount the massive positive, transformative influence this man made in my life over a decade ago, I can still hear his sincere voice, whether I was being praised or pushed, "Mike, I am for you."

Sales leader, if you've had a Steve Miller in your life, you immediately understand why I shared this personal story and why I exhort you to adopt this approach with your team members. And if you have not yet had the experience of being led by someone who was passionately *for you*, please know that you can absolutely make this type of impact in the lives of the people entrusted to your leadership.

ACHIEVE A QUADRUPLE WIN BY CONNECTING ON THE HEART LEVEL

Aside from the fact that actually caring about our people is *the right thing* to do, there is a wonderful business benefit that results when leaders are responsible stewards of the head and heart space we occupy—business results often dramatically improve.

I call this the Quadruple Win because there are four distinct parties who receive tremendous benefit when sales managers motivate their people to the max. Truly, everyone wins, except your competitor! Obviously, your salespeople win because connecting with them on this level drives full engagement. When their minds and hearts are laser locked on the mission, great things tend to happen and results skyrocket. The customer wins because they are working with a healthy, motivated salesperson that is being led (and even loved) well. Happy, fully engaged, driven sellers whose emotional needs are met are typically way better at meeting the needs of and delivering great value to customers. The third beneficiary is your company. Your highly effective leadership drives both top-line and bottom-line growth. Turnover goes down while productivity goes up. Your unemotional CFO will love the healthy P&L report generated by you connecting with the hearts of your sales team ☺. And finally, possibly the biggest winner of all is you, the sales manager. You not only experience the joy and satisfaction from seeing your life-giving leadership transforming your people, but they are going to produce killer results.

Sales leader, may the Quadruple Win inspire you to make the extra effort. *You*, and everyone else, will benefit. Your people crave something more than a quick check-in while passing in the hallway, a cheap text message, or a cursory email seeking some data point. Rather, you and they will reap the dividends when you connect with their heads and hearts, clearly communicating that you are *for them.*

FIVE SIMPLE TIPS TO ENGAGE HEARTS AND MINDS

I've got five really basic, yet proven, tips to help meet your people's need for attention and support and clearly communicate that you are for them. These simple efforts demonstrate that you care and that you're not just taking for granted the enormous bandwidth you occupy in their minds and their hearts.

1. **Pick up the phone, dial the numbers, and call them.** Not a text, not an email. Pick. Up. The. Phone. They need to hear your voice. Call for no other reason than to say hello and let them know that you're thinking about them and that you care. Voice trumps text. The phone call puts a person behind the outreach. Make. The. Call. Just like we do with people in our family or friends we actually care about. You don't even need to have an

agenda; it's more impactful when you don't. Just call to make a human connection.

2. **Stop putting off your proactive coaching time.** As described in chapter 4, one of our most critical jobs is helping our people get better at their jobs. What better way to respect the heart and head space we fill up in our people than to devote our precious time to investing in their improvement. Yet, as expressed earlier, proactive coaching is typically the first thing that sales managers cancel or postpone when the crap hits the fan. I know it is expedient to cancel fieldwork or a coaching session when something more urgent emerges, and at times, you may have to do so. But for goodness' sake, when that is the case, immediately get back to that salesperson to reschedule. If you postpone a coaching session or ride along and don't quickly reinitiate, this communicates lack of respect and care. If you had to cancel a date with your spouse, child, or friend because something urgent came up, wouldn't you demonstrate your sincere apology and good intent by immediately rescheduling with them? Don't cheat yourself or your people. Do your proactive coaching. Get it on your calendar and get with your people. It's not optional; it is your job.

3. **Show appreciation in a tangible and creative way.** Do something above the norm and personalize it. Again, add a human touch. Send a handwritten note. Send an old-fashioned card. Buy an inexpensive gift that represents your care for this individual—that you actually know their favorite hobby or interest. It could be something as simple and small as sending a magazine on a topic they follow or as generous as a gift card to their

favorite restaurant. Thoughtful gifts, regardless of cost, are underrated and often make a bigger and more lasting impact than we expect.

4. **Schedule a goal-setting session.** Ask each of your people to meet with you individually for a session focused on one thing—articulating their business and personal goals. Make it clear that you are interested in understanding what they want to achieve in the near and longer term, so you are able to provide the support and coaching to help them win. What better way to communicate you are *for* your salesperson than to make it clear that you're on their side? Again, I invoke Mike Jeffrey's exhortation for the manager to *become the bridge* between where the salesperson is today and where they want to be (who they want to become).

5. **Do something thoughtful, creative, and different for your next team meeting.** Take a field trip. Do a scavenger hunt. Meet at Topgolf or somewhere fun. One time I was working with a regional Bank of America executive who took the entire team to see an inspiring matinee movie and then out to dinner to share their takeaways. Months later the salespeople were still talking about that great experience and the lasting impact it made.

Sales managers take up way more emotional and mental bandwidth than we often appreciate. I say again, let's be great stewards of that high responsibility and neither abuse nor take for granted this powerful position. All four stakeholders of the Quadruple Win benefit greatly—the salesperson, the customer, the company, and you, the manager!

10

SLOW DOWN TO SPEED UP YOUR RAMP-UP

IN ALMOST ANY NEW VENTURE, getting off to a fast start is a universal desire. I mean, who doesn't want to get off to a fast start? Whether it's the new year, a new diet, a new hobby, or in this case, a new management role, we all want to start well and build momentum quickly.

You may have noticed, however, that through nine chapters of this book for first-time sales managers, there is nary a word about starting quickly. I promise, this is not an oversight. In fact, quite the opposite. I've previously shared my own frustrating experience about my first six months in sales management and in chapter 5 shared the pain and embarrassment that Meredith felt when she had to terminate two of her reps after sending them to President's Club because of her zeal, naivete, immaturity, and inexperience as a rookie manager.

Your zeal (and desire to start quickly as a first-time manager), while an admirable quality and possibly what helped land your new role, can actually work against you when taking on new leadership responsibility. It certainly did for Meredith and me.

As I was starting in my first sales management position, on paper, I looked like the perfect candidate. Having been the top producer in three different organizations and having just concluded a successful four-year stint in sales coaching and consulting, I was super confident that I knew exactly what to do as a new sales team leader. And the CEO who recruited me into the role was also supremely confident. I was chomping at the bit to get going and couldn't wait to jump in and immediately make my presence known. And because I was taking over an underperforming sales organization, I felt pressure to put my fingerprints on the culture and the sales process to make an impact as quickly as possible. Now looking back with the benefit of hindsight, however, I can see how my own excitement and the pressure I put on myself to start quickly were significant contributors to the slow, ineffective, discouraging, and frustrating launch of my sales management career.

It's a safe bet that you are looking to get off to a quick start too. This is probably one of the reasons you are reading this book. I get it—and that's exactly why this chapter offers yet one more piece of what feels like counterintuitive advice: slow down if you want to get off to a faster start! If you really want to speed up your ramp-up as a sales manager, the best coaching from the very best sales leaders is to slow down.

This topic has been percolating in the back of my mind while writing the previous chapters. As I've been outlining my thoughts, two particular sales leaders kept coming to mind.

TIPS FOR A FAST START FROM TWO INCREDIBLY TALENTED LEADERS WITH VERY DIFFERENT TENURES

Dennis Sorenson may be the single most strategic and driven senior sales leader on this planet. No client has stretched me further, forced me to raise my own game, or taught me more than Dennis has. His two guest appearances on my podcast drew rave reviews. He's a master at strategic selling, raising up leaders, and turning around sales organizations. For seven years I've benefited from our relationship and have had the privilege of watching Dennis lead people and dramatically grow sales. Supposedly I'm his coach and consultant, but I can argue it is actually the other way around—I'm convinced that I learn way more from him than he does from me.

The other sales leader I want to tell you about is on the other end of the tenure spectrum, barely six months into leading his first sales team. My relationship with Drew Ellis started when he sent me a LinkedIn thank-you message. He was not just complimentary but incredibly wise and insightful with his words. So much so that I asked him to hop online for a conversation so I could learn more about his successful start as a new sales leader. I was so impressed with Drew after that initial conversation, I did something that I had never done before—invited someone with whom I had not worked and did not know personally to be a guest on my show, confident that new sales leaders would benefit from hearing his story and approach. And am I glad I did. I'll share his story in a bit.

Back to Dennis. Having watched Dennis take on several new senior leadership assignments (and thrive) and also having benefited from observing his mentoring of newly promoted sales managers, I asked for his very best advice to help first-time managers get off to a fast and successful start. His response did not disappoint.

"Mike, I know this sounds like an oxymoron, but in order to go fast, new leaders need to slow down. They must slow down enough to spend time with each member of the team solely for the purpose of watching and listening. Asking great questions and truly 'listening to learn' are possibly the two most undervalued and underappreciated leadership skills. I strongly encourage every new team leader to go on a listening tour. See what type of work is being done. Observe. Ask lots of questions. Listen. Take in every bit of information you can."

What was fun about hearing Dennis preach this powerful wisdom to others is that I have witnessed him taking his own medicine and taking this exact approach himself. In fact, when he called me about a week after assuming his most recent role as the senior vice president of revenue and sales in a new company, one of the first things he said was that he would need a few months to really understand the lay of the land and to assess the talent on his new team and their needs before he could begin to draw up his plan for significant sales growth. When reminding Dennis that he shared this same principle with me two years ago, he offered a few more specifics for how he *goes slowly* during these early months.

Dennis says with a smile that Jeff Bezos of Amazon fame got it wrong in his book *Invent and Wander,* a collection of his writings. "Bezos says that we should 'invent and wander,' but I think that's backward. Leaders should wander then invent in response to what they see! Wander, get a feel, and let what you observe inform the plan you draft. Sure, you have ideas about your plan before your listening and observation tour, but I have seen time and time again that it is essential to let that early exposure to your team, and the business, *inform your plan*. Then you are really positioned well to introduce your new plan to team members so they can consume it and make it their own."

I just returned from participating in Dennis's annual sales kickoff meeting. It was a mind-blowing experience as I was able to witness firsthand the massive impact his leadership has made on that sales organization. Off all the kickoff meetings I attend across a wide variety of businesses every Q1, I don't remember ever seeing such an aligned, energized, and focused team. As strong and aggressive a growth leader Dennis is, it is his wisdom in selecting the right talent (chapter 6), his commitment to proactive coaching (chapter 4), and his strategic patience and willingness to listen and observe before implementing to which I credit his outrageous success.

While Dennis may be the strongest experienced sales leader I've encountered, Drew Ellis (recently promoted midmarket vice president for SAP) probably has the most conviction, discipline, and focus of any new sales leader I have met. I did not know of Drew until receiving that quite detailed thank-you note sharing about the excitement and success he was experiencing six months into his tenure in management. Curious to learn more, I asked him to speak with me. What was slotted for a twenty-minute intro conversation turned into almost an hour masterclass as this rookie manager regaled me with sales management best practice after best practice! Here is just a portion of what Drew shared with me in that initial conversation combined with his advice to help new managers get off to a fast start:

1. **Check your ego at the door.** You are no longer an individual contributor; you now must win through your team. That you may have been a top sales rep is not

enough to ensure greatness in a management role. This means not trying to be the team hero or the center of attention. It also means hiring people whom you believe might even be better than you, which certainly requires subduing your own ego. The quicker you check your ego, the faster you'll become effective as the sales leader.

2. **Commit to being great by consuming useful, practical content before assuming the role.** Drew consumed a massive amount of content before jumping into management. But he stresses that all great content is rooted in the fundamentals and seeks to simplify rather than complicate. He cautions against falling for gimmicks and shortcuts, and he offered up a phrase that I had not heard before: *fundamentals embarrass gimmicks*. All. Day. Long. So quickly get a firm grasp on the basics and avoid the trendy, gimmicky fluff at all costs.

3. **Build key frameworks as soon as possible.** Drew offered the example of studying and mastering my one-on-one accountability meeting framework (focusing on results then pipeline then activity, from chapter 3) before even starting in his management role. And once in the job, he quickly adapted and implemented it to fit the business he was leading.

4. **Build out cadences for high-impact tasks and activities.** Drew is a master of time blocking high-payoff activities, and he not only practices it himself, but he helps sales team members block critical new business development cadences into their calendars as well. He also maintains a schedule for his weekly and monthly accountability meetings, coaching sessions, team meeting prep sessions,

CRM maintenance sessions, prep time before forecast meetings with his senior management, and so on. Said more simply, Drew has full ownership of his most important sales management cadences and builds them into his calendar to ensure they happen.

5. **Hire for culture, grit, and fit.** I'm not sure I've heard a sales leader with greater conviction about the type of person he wants on his team than Drew. He is neither a sucker for bloviated résumé hyperbole nor interested in hiring people based on a beauty contest. He is intent on finding people who not only fit the role and the team but will fight to win!

6. **Spend time with other leaders (from inside and outside the company).** Drew recognizes the value he receives from regularly interacting with peer managers within his company, as well as partners and colleagues outside of the organization. The man is committed to being a lifetime learner always seeking to learn and incorporate principles and best practices from others.

More than any new manager I've encountered, Drew understands how overwhelming the job can become and has prepared and protected himself to thrive. When asked how he specifically prioritizes where to focus and how he shields his calendar from getting swallowed up by the unmanageable volume of requests and expectations that large companies often impose upon managers, he offered up two simple responses.

First, Drew religiously uses Eisenhower Charts to prioritize tasks. It is a methodology he first learned in college and one that he maintains to this day. The figure that follows depicts this most basic, tried-and-true tool. Drew regularly runs his tasks through this simple filter to decide which requests and tasks are worthy of attention. He is committed to not allowing the urgent to drown out the important and to avoiding or ignoring tasks that are neither important nor urgent. And he's committed to delegating tasks that require someone's attention (just not his) to others.

The second philosophy feeding Drew's insatiable hunger for prioritization and increased productivity is borrowed from retired Navy SEAL and author of the number one *New York Times* bestseller *Extreme Ownership*, Jocko Willink. In multiple conversations Drew referred to Willink's powerful phrase, *Discipline equals freedom*. Drew frees his mind by creating routines around his (and his team's) highest-impact activities (with a few key examples outlined in number four). These essential disciplines (like having sales reps time block dedicated hours for prospecting and proactive outreach) become sacrosanct;

these disciplines become established routines that ensure he, and his people, execute instead of just talk. He repeatedly emphasized that rather than making him feel constrained or trapped, his unwavering commitment to these routines produce a deep peace of mind and, as Willink promises, a sense of true freedom knowing that the most important tasks will be accomplished.

Drew summed up his philosophy quite simply. "Mike, discipline holds it all together."

INCREASED PRODUCTIVITY IS AS MUCH ABOUT WHAT YOU SAY NO TO

Over the past few years I have invested significant money and time studying productivity. Books. Online courses. In-person workshops. Podcasts. Mastermind groups. And more. My motivation was twofold. First, I was a mess. The growth of my business and the sheer volume of inquiries and opportunities on top of the day-to-day workload creating content, prepping for engagements, traveling to consult or speak, leading cohorts, hosting events, recording podcasts, and (poorly) attempting to keep up with social media notifications and messages (like the one Drew sent me) was simply overwhelming. Don't get me wrong; I'm not complaining. These are wonderful *challenges*, but that didn't make me feel any less overwhelmed or alter the reality that there are not enough hours in the day and week to juggle all of the work needing to be done.

The second motivation for gaining more mastery on the topic of productivity stemmed from what I was observing with my clients, and particularly with sales managers. The word *overwhelmed* is not strong enough to describe what so many managers are experiencing. Hundreds of emails. Getting pinged constantly with texts or other forms of instant messaging (Slack, Teams, and so on). Calendar invitations for back-to-back-to-back virtual meetings. Continual requests for fresh data or forecast updates. And all kinds of day-to-day low-value administrative tasks that seem to suck up whatever available time and oxygen remain.

Two key themes emerged from all of the productivity courses, books, and gurus. Get to your calendar first and block dedicated time for your highest-payoff activities. This ensures that there is always time committed to the precious few activities that truly move the needle and drive results. The second theme is the need to stay away from lower-value tasks that steal your time. Every productivity expert acknowledges that what you decide *not* to do is almost as important as deciding what you will do, because the obvious truth is that practically no one reading this book has a work-ethic problem. The answer to the productivity problem is not to work harder and to work more. Most sales managers are already working too much! Increasing productivity (and results) requires reallocating time from tasks that do not move the needle to those that do.

I am convinced that Drew Ellis's passion for discipline along with his firm grasp of the need to prioritize, even before taking on a management role, is one of the primary reasons that he has thrived as a new team leader. He has prepared himself to resist the universal principle often referred to as Parkinson's Law: work expands to fill the time allotted. Part of the reason I've woven the concept of productivity throughout this book is rooted in my belief that for you to win big as a new sales leader, you must win the battle for your time.

TO WIN BIG AS A NEW SALES LEADER, YOU MUST WIN THE BATTLE FOR YOUR TIME.

Honestly, as a coach, I would much rather preach philosophies and best practices for "how to" execute our most important behaviors. Believe me, it is much more fun helping salespeople sharpen their sales story, power up their prospecting, and perfect their probing. And with managers, it's more energizing modeling how to conduct a great accountability meeting or reviewing how to prepare team members for big sales calls. But the harsh truth is that if you are prevented from conducting the accountability meeting or coaching session because the well-intentioned but clueless people in your company keep piling more work on your desk and filling your inbox with trivial requests, it really doesn't matter how effective or brilliant you are at those high-payoff activities because you can't get to them!

Getting off to a solid start requires absolute clarity on which activities will help your team, and consequently you, win. And just to be exceedingly clear, winning here translates to your team achieving its goal and you setting up your life as sales manager in a sustainable manner.

Every task and request must be evaluated through the productivity lens. There will always be more work, often more than you could possibly do, even if you worked twenty-four hours per day. So perhaps First Lady Nancy Reagan had it right. *Just Say No* (if you were born after 1980, you can google it). Just because there was some task your predecessor in this position did, that does not mean that you have to do it. Just Say No. At the end of the day, or more accurately, at the end of the month, quarter, and year, you are going to be judged on the results your team produced. Therefore, the more time you spend on your two most important jobs, holding people accountable for producing results and helping them improve at producing results, the more success, the more fun, the more recognition you will achieve, and the greater your reward will be.

I'll add a few additional tips to Drew's advice. Tell people to stop copying you on every email they send to your salespeople. And instruct your salespeople to not copy you on emails unless you absolutely need to see what they are sending. Remember, the goal is to lead your team to sales victory, not to be involved in the minutia of every conversation and correspondence. There are no trophies awarded for processing the most emails, or even for getting to inbox zero once per week. There are certainly no prizes for destroying your home life because you've allowed people at your company who don't understand your priorities to bury you with things they may consider important but make no contribution to your team's success.

Let's wrap up this chapter back where we started it. Often it is our own passion that causes us to lose momentum before we hardly get started. In our intense desire to get off to a fast start and begin impacting the team and results, we tend to get ahead of ourselves. We quickly share our vision and plan to win and, without much thought, begin tackling every task put in front of us. Let me offer a sales coaching analogy that makes the point of this chapter exceedingly well. Generally speaking, when a salesperson is working a big, complex, important deal, the best advice to *speed up the sale* is to slow down the sales process. Instead of rushing to present and propose, true sales pros slow their roll. They make an extra effort to meet all the important stakeholders. They do extra discovery work to truly understand the customer's situation, challenges, needs, desired future state, and culture. They gather critical information that helps them shape the solution, and all the while, the extra investment they are making enhances the relationship with the customer, who now sees them as a patient professional and someone committed to their success.

My new manager friend, isn't that exactly what we want to accomplish with our teams? And isn't that the essence of Dennis Sorenson's exhortation that new managers need to slow down, go on a listening tour, and wander before inventing? I am convinced it is. To get off to a fast and successful start, heed the advice of the most driven sales leader I know. Slow down to speed up your ramp-up.

11

SALES MANAGEMENT SUCCESS IS DRIVEN BY MASTERY OF THE FUNDAMENTALS, NOT FANCY TOYS AND TRICKS

I HAVE THE SENSE THAT AFTER consuming the first ten chapters you are not surprised by the title and theme of this concluding one: fundamentals, not fancy tricks.

But before sending you off with one last blast of encouragement and a benediction, let me pause for a moment to express my sincere gratitude and appreciation. I never take for granted when extremely busy, often-overloaded individuals invest their most precious, scarce resource to consume my content. Whether it's a short article, a podcast episode, or an entire book like this one, I do not take your investment of time, or the opportunity cost of sacrificing something else, lightly. So, thank you. Deep, heartfelt thanks for entrusting me and *The First-Time Manager: Sales* with your time and focus.

• • •

SALES MANAGERS AND SALES TEAMS DON'T FAIL BECAUSE THEY LACK A COOL NEW TOOL OR PROCESS

As you wrap up reading and begin implementing your takeaways from the book, allow me to restate this critical truth lest you be tempted to cut corners and seek out *easy* fixes: There. Are. No. Shortcuts. The answer to your sales management challenge is not a hack found in a trending article on LinkedIn (likely written by some sales consultant wannabe blogging from his mother's basement).

I promise you that the answer to your sales problem is not a quick fix. There is no secret sauce. Trust me, we've all searched for a magic bullet. It. Doesn't. Exist. Please believe me when I shout with all my being that, for all of the sales organizations I've been around for the past few decades, not once have I seen a sales leader or a sales team fail because they were lacking some new tool, toy, or process. Similar to my fantasy that this year's latest driver model will transform my golf game, there is no one trick to guarantee outrageous success as a new manager. So save yourself the wasted time and the disappointment, avoid the clickbait, hype, and false promises, and don't even entertain your FOMO that there's some perfect easy fix to be discovered.

FOCUS ON THESE FUNDAMENTALS

One last time I exhort you to adopt and master the one-on-one accountability meeting as described in chapter 3. The single most important thing you can do to establish and maintain a winning culture and drive increased results is to hold your people accountable for doing their jobs. Never, even for a moment, allow the thought to creep in that anything about accountability for delivering results is unkind, immoral, or politically incorrect. In fact, not holding people accountable for performance is the height of irresponsibility as the sales team leader because sales is, after all, about results. The framework from chapter 3 provides a foolproof approach to ensure you will radically increase accountability without micromanaging or demotivating your team members. Deploy that approach and you and your team will reap the rewards.

Your next most important job is helping your salespeople improve at their job. There is no better way to spend available discretionary sales management time than working with and alongside your people. Resist the temptation to postpone or cancel proactive coaching time with your sellers when confronted with *urgent requests* that supposedly need your immediate attention. This may sound like an oxymoron, but the urgent requests can wait! Trust me, new urgent requests for the frontline sales manager emerge on a daily basis. If you continually put off working with and coaching your people until every daily fire is extinguished, you will truly never get around to coaching (and results will suffer).

After mastering accountability and coaching, sharpening your focus on the various aspects of talent management will not only drive more results, but you'll enjoy your life as a sales manager significantly more when you

- get the right people on your team,
- spend more time with your very best people, and
- more quickly identify and address underperformance.

One final reminder that though we are often not aware of the extent to which this is true, managers take up a ton more space in our salespeople's minds and hearts than we typically realize. It is indeed a powerful position we hold, which presents an enormous opportunity to use all that mental and emotional bandwidth we occupy for everyone's good. The more effectively we communicate and demonstrate to our people that we are for them, the more receptive to our pushing, stretching, challenging, and coaching they will be.

I WOULD BE HONORED TO CONTINUE TO SUPPORT YOU

It is time to wish you well in your sales management journey, so let's finish right back where we began. Congratulations! You have been entrusted with what I believe is one of the most important jobs in the business world. You are positioned to make a tremendous impact on the business, and the lives, sales success, and careers of the people on your team, as well as your own success, earnings, and career path.

I am excited for you and would be honored to continue to support you along your sales leadership journey. I would also be remiss if I did not point you to my three most popular resources to help increase sales and sales management effectiveness:

- The *Sales Management. Simplified Podcast* (listen on my site at mikeweinberg.com/podcast or find the show on your favorite podcast provider)
- *Sales Management. Simplified: The Straight Truth About Getting Exceptional Results from Your Sales Team*
- *New Sales. Simplified: The Essential Handbook for Prospecting and New Business Development*

BONUS RESOURCE

There are more resources, including my blog, at mikeweinberg.com; and feel free to connect with me on social channels at @mike_weinberg. I would love to track with your future success.

Wishing you much success, great sales leadership, and to your sales team, tons of New Sales!

Mike

INDEX

ABOUT THE AUTHOR

MIKE WEINBERG'S passion is helping sellers and sales teams Win More New Sales. His specialties are sales management and new business development.

Mike was the #1 salesperson in three organizations prior to launching his own business, and he is the author of three previous bestselling books—*New Sales. Simplified*, *Sales Management. Simplified*, and *Sales Truth*.

Known for his blunt, funny, tell-it-like-it-is approach, Mike's simple, practical, powerful, easy-to-implement concepts are appreciated by salespeople, sales leaders, and executives. He's spoken on five continents and has become one of the most trusted and sought-after sales speakers/trainers in the world. Mike works with companies in all industries ranging in size from a few million to many billions of dollars.

A native New Yorker, Mike is always on the hunt for the best New York pizza wherever his travels take him, and he is a huge golf and Porsche 911 fan. Mike and his wife, Katie, call St. Louis home and have three young adult children and one new granddaughter.